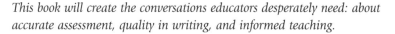

This book will create the conversations educators desperately need: about accurate assessment, quality in writing, and informed teaching.

—RANDY BOMER, AUTHOR OF *TIME TO LEARN: CRAFTING LITERATE LIVES IN MIDDLE & HIGH SCHOOL*

Reading Wilson's book feels like joining an exciting conversation in the staff lunchroom with a new colleague. She radiates energy, wit, and passion in her discussion of literacy education. Her considerable expertise in the concrete realities of teaching writing in school matches her knowledge in the history and theory of writing assessment. Even more important, she grounds her work in a powerful ethical commitment, challenging her readers and herself to teach and assess writing closer to the way we know we should, even as she helps us grapple with practical constraints like the time crunch and the need to give grades at mid-term. One of the most nervy and gutsy thinkers and writers I've read lately, Wilson fearlessly challenges established educational leaders and authors. Rarely have I encountered a writer who can move so effortlessly—and entertainingly—from lively classroom stories and detailed evaluations of students' texts to conceptual innovations and visionary proposals for change.

—BOB BROAD, AUTHOR OF *WHAT WE REALLY VALUE: BEYOND RUBRICS IN TEACHING AND ASSESSING WRITING*

Rethinking Rubrics in Writing Assessment *is a must read for all classroom teachers who have rebelled against fitting their students' wild and wonderful writing into tiny boxes—and for those who haven't rebelled yet. Maja Wilson's delightful mix of classroom stories and research makes a powerful argument against the sacred cow of writing rubrics.*

—LINDA CHRISTENSEN, AUTHOR OF *READING, WRITING, AND RISING UP: TEACHING ABOUT SOCIAL JUSTICE AND THE POWER OF THE WRITTEN WORD*

Education has largely been reduced to rubrics. In Rethinking Rubrics in Writing Assessment, *Maja Wilson explores the cause and the cost of this reduction. She begins with her own teaching dilemmas and her refusal to reduce a student's writing to the dimensions of a rubric. Through incisive examples, metaphors, and humor, Wilson shows us the shackles of rubrics then helps us break them. This book is not just for people interested in writing assessment, but for anyone concerned about children and their education. The book is superbly written. I couldn't put it down.*

—PETER JOHNSTON, AUTHOR OF *KNOWING LITERACY: CONSTRUCTIVE LITERACY ASSESSMENT*

RETHINKING RUBRICS IN WRITING ASSESSMENT

MAJA WILSON

HEINEMANN
PORTSMOUTH, NH

Heinemann
361 Hanover Street
Portsmouth, NH 03801–3912
www.heinemann.com

Offices and agents throughout the world

Library of Congress Cataloging-in-Publication Data
Wilson, Maja.
    Rethinking rubrics in writing assessment / Maja Wilson.
      p. cm.
    Includes bibliographical references and index.
    ISBN 0-325-00856-6 (alk. paper)
    1. English language—Composition and exercises—Study and
teaching—United States—Evaluation. I. Title.
    LB1576.W48887 2006
    372.62'3—dc22   2005026599

Editor: Gloria Pipkin
Production: Patricia Adams
Typesetter: Gina Poirier Design
Cover design: Night and Day Design
Manufacturing: Steve Bernier

Printed in the United States of America on acid-free paper
10   09   08   VP   2   3   4   5

To Gloria Pipkin.

This book was her idea, and I wish for all of our students the kind of conversations about writing and life that I have known with her.

Contents

Acknowledgments

Thanks to my family: to Patrick, whose admonishment to finish the book and "Just do like this!" as he air-typed wildly always made me laugh; to Isaiah and Wavy, who sacrificed their mother for an entire year against their will for the sake of the future of writing assessment; to my mother, who always found me a book to read; to my father, who read and responded to my childhood writings; to my sister Amy, who enthusiastically suffered through early drafts of this manuscript; and to my sister Judy, who teaches against the odds.

Every writer has a weakness. I have many, but the lovely Ms. Thistlebottom managed to keep most of my structures parallel and my commas safely tucked inside the quotation marks. I shall never be able to repay her.

Teaching can be a lonely profession. My friend and colleague Amy Marsh has made it less so. Amy's intelligence, compassion, and sense of humor have kept me sane. If this book is made into a movie, she would like to be played by Oprah. I am thankful to my colleagues Dale, Keith, Laura, Jon, Jim, Dana, Kristin, and Jenny for their dedication to teaching and for their willingness to hire me.

I appreciate the generous feedback to early versions of this book that saved me from myself. Thoughtful and honest responses from Wendell Ricketts, Lind Williams, Bob Broad, Susan Ohanian, Patricia Lynne, and Peter Simons have helped to untangle me from several knots I wrote myself into and strengthened the manuscript considerably.

I also appreciate the influence of my poetry professor Paul McGlynn, whose rants against lovely words and lovely drinks have steered me mostly clear of cliché and cocktail umbrellas.

Acknowledgments for a book about writing wouldn't be complete without a nod to my earliest writing partner and critic, Sarah Manney, who uncomplainingly read more than her fair share of poetry about my adolescent angst.

A special thanks to Krystal Aguilar, Denni Agens, and Maria Haramboure, whose writing appears in this book, as well as all the members of my Personal Narratives class. Their words make it well worth the work.

Foreword

by Alfie Kohn

Once upon a time I vaguely thought of assessment in dichotomous terms: The old approach, which consisted mostly of letter grades, was crude and uninformative, while the new approach, which included things like portfolios and rubrics, was detailed and authentic. Only much later did I look more carefully at the individual floats rolling by in the alternative assessment parade—and stop cheering.

For starters, I realized that it's hardly sufficient to recommend a given approach on the basis of its being better than old-fashioned report cards. By that criterion, just about anything would look good. I eventually came to understand that not all alternative assessments are authentic. My growing doubts about rubrics in particular were prompted by the assumptions on which this technique rested and also the criteria by which they (and assessment itself) were typically judged. These doubts were stoked not only by murmurs of dissent I heard from thoughtful educators[1] but by the case made *for* this technique by its enthusiastic proponents. For example, I read in one article that "rubrics make assessing student work quick and efficient, and they help teachers to justify to parents and others the grades that they assign to students."[2] To which the only appropriate response is: Uh-oh.

I had been looking for an alternative to grades, and the reason I was keen to find one is that research shows three reliable effects when students are graded: They tend to think less deeply, avoid taking risks, and lose interest in the learning itself.[3] The ultimate goal of authentic assessment must be the elimination of grades. Obviously, a strategy that merely offered a new way to arrive at those final marks wouldn't address the fundamental problem of students who had been led to focus on getting As (or their equivalent) rather than on making sense of ideas. Moreover, something that was commended to teachers as a handy strategy of self-justification during parent conferences ("Look at all these 3s, Mrs. Grommet! How could I have given Zach anything but a B?") didn't seem particularly promising for inviting teachers to rethink their practices and premises.

As for the selling point of "quick and efficient," I've graded enough student papers to understand the appeal of this promise. Still, the best teachers would react with skepticism, if not disdain. They'd immediately ask what we had to sacrifice in order to spit out a series of tidy judgments about the quality of student learning. To ponder that question is to understand how something that presents itself as an innocuous scoring guide can be so profoundly wrongheaded.

The first problem is that the how's of assessment (when they preoccupy us) chase the why's back into the shadows. So let's shine a light over there and ask: What's our reason for trying to evaluate the quality of students' efforts? This is a question we rarely ask, but it matters whether the objective is to (1) rank kids against one another, (2) provide an extrinsic inducement for them to try harder, or (3) offer feedback that will help them become more adept at, and excited about, what they're doing. I worry that giving teachers more efficient rating techniques—and imparting a scientific luster to those ratings—may make it even easier to avoid asking this question. In any case, it's certainly not going to shift our rationale away from (1) or (2) and toward (3).

Second, consistent and uniform standards are admirable, and maybe even workable, when we're talking about, say, the manufacture of DVD players. The process of trying to gauge children's understanding of ideas is a very different matter, however, and ought to be treated as such. It necessarily entails the exercise of human judgment, which is a messy, imprecise, subjective affair. Rubrics are, above all, a tool to promote standardization, to turn teachers into grading machines or at least allow them to pretend that what they're doing is efficient, exact, and objective. Frankly, I'm amazed by the number of educators whose opposition to standardized tests and standardized curricula mysteriously fails to extend to standardized in-class assessments.

The appeal of rubrics is supposed to be their high interrater reliability, finally delivered to language arts—the "transformation of English classes into something as rigorous and legitimate as biology or chemistry classes," as Maja Wilson puts it. A list of criteria for what should be awarded the highest possible score when evaluating an essay is supposed to reflect near-unanimity on the part of the people who designed the rubric and is supposed to assist all those who use it to figure out (that is, to discover rather than to decide) which essays meet those criteria.

Now some observers criticize rubrics because they can never deliver the promised precision; judgments ultimately turn on adjectives that are murky and end up being left to the teacher's discretion. But I worry more about the success of rubrics than their failure. Just as it's possible to raise standardized test scores, providing that you're willing to gut the curriculum and turn the school into a test-preparation factory, it's possible to get a bunch of people to agree on what rating to give an assignment, providing that they're willing to accept and apply someone else's narrow criteria for what merits that rating. Once we check our judgment at the door, we can all learn to give a 4 to exactly the same things.

This attempt to deny the subjectivity of human judgment, this "fear of disagreement," as Wilson calls it, is objectionable in its own right. But it's also harmful in a very practical sense. In an important article published in 1999, Linda Mabry, now at Washington State University, pointed out that rubrics "are designed to function as scoring guidelines, but they also serve as arbiters of quality and agents of control" over what is taught and valued. Because "agreement among scorers is more easily achieved with regard to such matters as spelling and organization," these are the characteristics that will likely find favor in a rubricized classroom. Mabry cites research showing that "compliance with the rubric tended to yield higher scores but produced 'vacuous' writing."[4]

To this point, my objections assume only that teachers rely on rubrics to standardize the way they think about student assignments. Despite my misgivings, I can imagine a scenario where teachers benefit from consulting a rubric briefly in the early stages of designing a curriculum unit in order to think about various criteria by which to assess what students end up doing. As long as the rubric is only one of several sources, as long as it doesn't drive the instruction, it could conceivably play a constructive role.

But all bets are off if *students* are given the rubrics and asked to navigate by them. The proponent I quoted earlier, who boasted of efficient scoring and convenient self-justification, also wants us to employ these guides so that students will know ahead of time exactly how their projects will be evaluated. In support of this proposition, a girl who didn't like rubrics is quoted as complaining, "If you get something wrong, your teacher can prove you knew what you were supposed to do."[5] Here we're invited to have a good laugh at this student's expense. The implication is that kids' dislike of these things proves their usefulness—a kind of "gotcha" justification.

Just as standardizing assessment for teachers may compromise the quality of teaching, so standardizing assessment for learners may compromise the learning. Mindy Nathan, a Michigan teacher and former school board member told me that she began "resisting the rubric temptation" the day "one particularly uninterested student raised his hand and asked if I was going to give the class a rubric for this assignment." She realized that her students, presumably grown accustomed to rubrics in other classrooms, now seemed "unable to function unless every required item is spelled out for them in a grid and assigned a point value. Worse than that," she added, "they do not have confidence in their thinking or writing skills and seem unwilling to really take risks."[6]

This is the sort of outcome that may not be noticed by an assessment specialist who is essentially a technician, in search of practices that yield data in ever-greater quantities. A B+ at the top of a paper tells a student very little about its quality, whereas a rubric provides more detailed information based on multiple criteria. Therefore, a rubric is a superior assessment.

The fatal flaw here is revealed by a line of research in educational psychology showing that students whose attention is relentlessly focused on how well they're doing often become less engaged with *what* they're doing. There's a big difference between thinking about the content of a story one is reading (for example, trying to puzzle out why a character made a certain decision), and thinking about one's own proficiency at reading. "Only extraordinary education is concerned with learning," the writer Marilyn French once observed, whereas "most is concerned with achieving: and for young minds, these two are very nearly opposites."[7] In light of this distinction, it's shortsighted to assume that an assessment technique is valuable in direct proportion to how much information it provides. At a minimum, this criterion misses too much.

But the news is even worse than that. Studies have shown that too much attention to the quality of one's performance is associated with more superficial thinking, less interest in whatever one is doing, less perseverance in the face of failure, and a tendency to attribute results to innate ability and other factors thought to be beyond one's control.[8] To that extent, more detailed and frequent evaluations of a student's accomplishments may be downright counterproductive. As one sixth grader put it, "The whole time I'm writing, I'm not thinking about what I'm saying or how I'm saying it. I'm worried about what grade the teacher will give me, even if she's handed out a rubric. I'm more focused on being correct than on being honest in my writing."[9] In many cases, the word *even* in that second sentence might be replaced with *especially*. But, in this respect at least, rubrics aren't uniquely destructive. Any form of assessment that encourages students to keep asking, "How am I doing?" is likely to change how they look at themselves and at what they're learning, usually for the worse.

The book you're about to read is not only a superb analysis of rubrics but a lesson in how to apply careful thinking to classroom practice. There is an inviting informality to Wilson's tone that manages to coexist with incisive analysis and careful organization. She's persuasive by virtue of her arguments and experience, without a hint of pomposity—and she makes all this look effortless.

What really distinguishes Wilson's analysis is her willingness to challenge rubrics not merely for their technical deficiencies but on the basis of the goals they serve. That's a rarity in the world of assessment. She contends that improving the design of rubrics, or even inventing our own, will not suffice because there are problems inherent to the very idea of rubrics. She shows that their attempt to standardize assessment is rooted in an effort to rank students against one another—and she points out that neither we nor our assessment strategies can be simultaneously devoted to helping all students improve *and* to sorting them into winners and losers.

What seems to trouble Wilson most of all, though, is how rubrics are relentlessly reductive (a fact that can drive anyone to alarming alliteration). High scores on a list of criteria for good writing do not mean that what has been written is good, she explains, because quality is more than the sum of its rubricized parts. In fact, she suggests in passing that "we need to look to the piece of writing itself to suggest its own evaluative criteria"—a truly radical and provocative suggestion.

Wilson also makes the devastating observation that a relatively recent "shift in writing pedagogy has not translated into a shift in writing assessment." Teachers are given much more sophisticated and progressive guidance nowadays about how to teach writing but are still told to pigeonhole the results, to quantify what can't really be quantified. Thus, the dilemma, which she doesn't shrink from describing, just as she doesn't hesitate to identify by name who's leading us astray: Either our instruction and our assessment remain "out of sync" or the instruction gets worse in order that students' writing can be easily judged with the help of rubrics.

I love that Wilson is not only willing but able to think seriously about alternatives—that is, ways of evaluating writing that are grounded in her classroom experience and consistent with the values that inform her critique. The result is a book that I dearly hope will be read not only among people who teach writing (and think about teaching writing, and think about teaching writing to writing teachers), but among people whose specialty is assessment.

Rethinking Rubrics is, at its core, a rather incendiary piece of work. But then, as the late John Nicholls once remarked in response to my use of that word to describe another education book, "There's a lot of trash to be burnt."

Notes

[1] In addition to the sources I'm about to cite, I might mention critical comments about rubrics offered by Bruce Marlowe and Marilyn Page (in *Creating and Sustaining the Constructivist Classroom*, 2nd ed., [Thousand Oaks, CA: Corwin, 2005], p. 56); Susan Ohanian (in *What Happened to Recess and Why Are Our Children Struggling in Kindergarten?* [New York: McGraw-Hill, 2002], p. 40); Jackie Brooks (as quoted by Kathy Checkley, "Assessment That Serves Instruction," *ASCD Education Update*, June 1997, p. 5); and Dennis Littky (as quoted by Eliot Levine, *One Kid at a Time* [New York: Teachers College Press, 2002], p. 116). Also, assessment specialist W. James Popham ("What's Wrong—and What's Right—with Rubrics," *Educational Leadership*, October 1997, pp. 72–75) faults many rubrics for being overly detailed and for using criteria that are amorphous, if not tautological.

[2] Heidi Goodrich Andrade, "Using Rubrics to Promote Thinking and Learning," *Educational Leadership*, February 2000, p. 13.

[3] I review this research in *Punished by Rewards* (Boston: Houghton Mifflin, 1993) and *The Schools Our Children Deserve* (Boston: Houghton Mifflin, 1999), as well as in "From Degrading to De-Grading," *High School Magazine*, March 1999 (available at *www.alfiekohn.org/teaching/fdtd-g.htm*).

[4] Linda Mabry, "Writing to the Rubric," *Phi Delta Kappan*, May 1999, pp. 678, 676.

[5] Quoted by Andrade, "Understanding Rubrics," in *http://learnweb .harvard.edu/alps/thinking/docs/rubricar.htm.* Another educator cites this same quotation and adds: "Reason enough to give rubrics a closer look!" It's also quoted on the RubiStar website, which is a sort of online rubric-o-matic.

[6] Mindy Nathan, personal communication, October 26, 2004. As a student teacher, Nathan was disturbed to find that her performance, too, was evaluated by means of a rubric that offered a ready guide for evaluating instructional "competencies." In an essay written at the end of her student-teaching experience, she commented, "Of course, rubrics don't lie; they just don't tell the whole story. They crunch a semester of shared learning and love into a few squares on a sheet that can make or break a career." That's why she vowed, "I won't do this to my students. My goal as a teacher will be to preserve and present the human aspects of my students that defy rubric-ization."

[7] Marilyn French, *Beyond Power: On Women, Men, and Morals* (New York: Summit, 1985), p. 387.

[8] For more on the distinction between performance and learning—and the detrimental effects of an excessive focus on performance—see *The Schools Our Children Deserve*, chap. 2, which reviews research by Carol Dweck, Carole Ames, Carol Midgley, John Nicholls, and others.

[9] Quoted in Natalia Perchemlides and Carolyn Coutant, "Growing Beyond Grades," *Educational Leadership*, October 2004, p. 54. Notice that this student is actually making two separate points. Even some critics of rubrics, who are familiar with the latter objection—that honesty may suffer when technical accuracy is overemphasized—seem to have missed the former one.

Introduction

When Best Practice and Our Deepest Convictions Are at Odds

*More often than not . . . the field of composition has erred when
it has too hastily trusted and laid claim to certainty. . . .
Instead of providing solutions, the urge for certainty has often
created new problems by encouraging simpleminded mechanical
procedures for teaching or learning highly complex skills and
processes. Guised in the cloak of reliability and efficiency, such
procedures are instructionally very attractive, and teachers adopt
them rapidly, often in spite of their deepest convictions about the
complexities of the writing process.*

—CHRIS ANSON (1989, 2)

Amy's Ford Pinto is packed with far too many clothes and coolers for
a three-day weekend at her family's cottage, but that doesn't stop us
from driving back to Jenny's house for the coffee maker, just in case.
We'd hate to be stuck on a writing weekend without coffee. As Jenny
climbs back into the car, balancing the coffee maker on the four lap-
tops piled next to me, I mention how funny it would be for the math
teachers in our district to get together over the summer for a math
weekend. As we laugh at the image, Amy says in all sincerity, "We
have the coolest subject."

Later that day, as Amy writes about nakedness and Laura curses
Emily Dickinson and Jenny blurs the line between Harlequin
Romance and personal narrative, I think about my deepest convictions about writing: about the magic of developing and finding a
voice, about the constant struggle to meaningfully represent experience through words. I think about Frederick Douglass, whose literacy
literally and metaphorically saved his life. I think about Maya
Angelou, whose conviction about the power of words drove her to
silence before it emerged in all the beauty of her writing. I think

about Emily Dickinson, who wouldn't go outside, but whose words have traveled through space and time and a certain slant of light. I think about my students, who wonder if words can carry the weight of their convictions and fears. And I think that Amy is right; English is the coolest subject.

Writing teachers are a passionate group. Our earliest and deepest experiences with language led us to this profession. We were seduced by the rhythm of language, or by the connection stories brought us with our parents, or by the way words allowed us to form and express our humanity. We were comforted by the way that writing anchored our thoughts on paper, allowing us to build solid ideas from fluid thoughts. We were amazed by the way that scribbles on paper could create understanding. We are convinced that there is something fundamentally sacred about teaching writing—about helping another person to express and shape their humanity through language.

Still, I think of the huge no man's land between my deeply held convictions about the power of writing and some of my classroom practices. I remember with a sinking feeling the quiz I gave in which I asked students to list the steps of the writing process and then define the word *recursive*. I remember the time Tim didn't know what to write next and I gave him an entire sentence instead of asking him questions to prompt his own words. I tell this to Amy in order to dispense with my guilt, and she admits to similar transgressions: the paper hastily graded, the writing starter quickly lifted from the book of canned journal prompts, the empty praise offered in a moment of weakness. We know that good teachers must constantly revisit their knowledge about best practice and question their performance in light of this knowledge, and we are comforted that at least we know when we fall short. It will take a lifetime to become good teachers, and we can accept our shortcomings as long as we are headed in the right direction.

What happens, however, when the field of writing methods leads us astray? For the most part, the things we learn from methods classes, *English Journal* articles, or professional conferences work well; no one would argue that using writing as punishment really works or that giving feedback only on spelling errors has been mistakenly questioned. But imagine our dismay when we adopt a practice faithfully and it turns out to be a dead end or to create more problems than it solves. What if a practice touted as best violates our "deepest convictions about the complexities of the writing process?"

Just as reflective teachers must question their own performance, we must be willing to question the methods accepted as best by the field of writing methods, an idea that may strike us as sacrilege. The very words *best practice* are loaded; if we aren't following best practice, aren't we by extension following worst practice? In addition, the term drips with authority. We may imagine that the process of determining best practice is mysterious but vaguely scientific; we picture labs with student control groups and teacher researchers in white coats behind one-way mirrors taking copious notes. We may assume that methods destined for the best practice label must undergo rigorous testing akin to the FDA or ADA processes of approval.

Our mental association of the term *best practice* with a doctor's white lab coat and its aura of infallibility is no accident. In the preface to their book *Best Practice: New Standards for Teaching and Learning in America's Schools*, Steven Zemelman, Harvey Daniels, and Arthur Hyde (1998) explain the origins of the term in education. In the late 1980s and early 1990s these authors were concerned that the school reform movement in Chicago would ignore important "issues of teaching and learning." They received a grant from the Joyce Foundation to create a newspaper focused on instruction, a newspaper they named *Best Practice 1*.

> Why did we adopt the term "Best Practice," first for our newspaper and now for this book? We borrowed the expression, of course, from the professions of medicine and law, where "good practice" and "best practice" are everyday phrases used to describe solid, reputable, state-of-the-art work in a field. If a practitioner is following best practice standards, he or she is aware of current research and consistently offers clients the full benefits of the latest knowledge, technology, and procedures. If a doctor, for example, does not follow contemporary standards and a case turns out badly, peers may criticize his or her decisions and treatments by saying something like, "that was simply not best practice." (vii–viii)

Since the starting teacher salary at my public school is less than two hundred dollars higher than Salary Wizard's estimation of the average starting salary of a light truck driver in a city near mine, I understand Zemelman, Hyde, and Daniels' urge to link our work with the work of doctors and lawyers. Perhaps this association could lend us a measure of the respect and pay we're surely due. But we would be wise to examine our metaphors lest they lead us to a place we never intended to go. The authority conferred upon educational best practice by its association with the medical field has far-reaching implications. The No Child Left Behind Act calls for closing the achievement gap using "effective, scientifically based instructional strategies" (Public Law 107–110, Section 1001, (9)). Like drugs, if teaching strategies, methods, and assessments can be proven effective in clinical trials, don't we want them administered properly and consistently? If a doctor can be sued for failing to order a CAT scan when indicated, shouldn't teachers be held accountable for dispensing proven methods?

Best practice, then, becomes a supporting argument for mandating increasingly specific practices. Throughout New York City's Public School Region 10 in 2005, English language arts (ELA) teachers were required to display books in crates cover side out. Literacy Coaches at Intermediate School (IS) 172 did sporadic checks, reprimanding the unruly teacher who might have had the audacity to store her books in a bookcase spine side out. It's hard to argue with the good sense in displaying books in crates cover side out; besides being aesthetically pleasing, such an arrangement makes books more visible. And book crates are definitely more portable than bookcases; imagine all the possible exciting configurations! The problem comes when this arrangement is enforced. "I spend too much of my prep period arranging and rearranging my class library," says my sister Judy, an ELA teacher at IS 172. "I'd rather spend my time reading young adult literature so I can match books with my students." But forget the power of a well-timed book suggestion; conclusions from the studies on personal recommendation aren't in yet.

If only good teaching were as easy as following an approved list of prescriptions. Unfortunately, children are not bacteria to be obliterated by the correct dose of penicillin, and classes are not control groups whose every variable can be isolated. Since human beings are complex and class dynamics often surprising, teachers must be free to explore a wide range of possible approaches. Imagine the difference to teachers at IS 172 if the term *best practice* had been changed to *promising practice*. While the word *best* assumes a fixed canon of methods and closes off the possibility of other ways, the word *promising* offers the possibility of exploration. The question would no longer be, "Are you following best practice?" but "Are you exploring, discovering, and creating practices with promise?"

Even if we accept the medical model of mandating proven methods, we cannot be bullied into accepting the scientific infallibility of best practice; the blind acceptance of best practice in medicine has sometimes ended in disaster. Consider Thalidomide. By the 1960s, doctors in Europe and Canada regularly prescribed Thalidomide to pregnant women to help them with morning sickness. Studies indicated that the drug, unlike barbiturates, could be administered without toxic side effects. Although the first reported "Thalidomide baby" was born with severely deformed ears in 1956, it was not until 1961 when a German doctor determined that 50 percent of children born with deformities had been exposed to Thalidomide in the first trimester of pregnancy that countries began to pull the drug from the market.

Certainly, no teaching method that currently enjoys the label of best practice will result in death or deformity, at least of the body. The example of Thalidomide as it illustrates the argument for skepticism of best practice in education is hyperbole. But its legacy should give teachers the courage to question best practice.

If it is true that the field of writing methods can lead us astray, and if it is true that we cannot blindly accept teaching methods touted as "best," how do we know which daily practices to question? We certainly don't have time to investigate every study published for every classroom practice we have ever tried. Perhaps, as Chris Anson (1989) suggests, we can begin by questioning practices that violate our "deepest convictions about the complexities of the writing process."

However, in the middle of the school year, it is easy to forget to reflect on our deepest convictions about the complexities of the writing process. The school systems in which we teach do not consider reflection to be a part of our job. Besides study hall duty, lunch duty, school improvement duty, curriculum council duty, and our own personal duty to use the restroom at least once a week, our job is to usher over one hundred students in and out of our rooms every day, to prepare them for state writing tests, the AP test, the ACT, the SAT, tomorrow's unit test, the real world, and adulthood. Without time to think and reflect on why we began teaching English in the first place, our daily practices are vulnerable to the demands of local, state, and national politics—demands that may have nothing to do with the reasons and ways that human beings connect powerfully with language. If we are to create the conditions in which our students can experience the rich power of language, we must constantly remind ourselves of our own deepest convictions about writing. Once we remember these, identifying practices that violate these convictions is the easy part.

You have probably picked up this book because something about rubrics violates your deepest convictions about the complexities of the writing process. If so, your misgivings have likely had little validation. While leaders in the field of writing assessment such as Patricia Lynne, Bob Broad, and Brian Huot have done invaluable work in pushing writing assessment at the university level beyond the limits of rubrics, I've not encountered a single book or article intended for K through 12 writing teachers that critiques rubrics. Without validation, our misgivings fade into resignation. *Rethinking Rubrics* is an attempt to articulate and explore how rubrics may violate the complexities of the writing process so that we can begin our search for more promising practices.

My Troubles with Rubrics

*I collect rubrics. I love them. They are as dear to me
as beanie babies, barbie dolls, mugs, key chains,
NCTE memorabilia, and dust bunnies under my bed.*

—KIT GORRELL (1998)

My introduction to rubrics came in second grade when my swim teacher used a series of statements in nifty boxes to assess my front crawl and elementary backstroke. I remember proudly reading the phrases and numbers praising the grace of my strokes to my mother and pitying the poor children whose flutter kicks were still progressing, understanding even then that the low numbers attached to the these boxes belied their euphemistic phrasing. Rubrics followed me into teacher training and beyond. I still obsess over why my student teacher performance rubric rated my classroom management skills as "adequate" rather than "excellent." Did I not use proximity and make eye contact with misbehaving students? Did I not flick the lights on and off as a last resort? When I became a new teacher in Michigan, I was quickly introduced to the four-point rubric used by the Michigan Educational Assessment Program (MEAP) to assess student writing, and was just as quickly introduced to the MEAP's six-point rubric when it changed the following year. I once promised my students several bonus points if they would simply staple the process paper rubric I had distributed to their final how-to drafts. I have been asked during several interviews if I can effectively use rubrics. Not only can I effectively use rubrics, but I also cannot escape them.

Like any other idea in education that can be expressed in a spreadsheet, rubrics have been co-opted for profit; textbooks and canned instruction programs come complete with pre-made assessment rubrics. I typed www.rubric.com in the address box of my browser, and was pleased not only to learn everything I ever wanted to know about the joys of rubrics, but I was also able to download The Rubricator™, a software program that would allow me to quickly create my own rubric, link performance tasks to any national standard, and choose between many pleasing layouts at the click of an icon. All for only $29.95, last time I checked. At a recent National Council of Teachers of English (NCTE) conference, I was invited by a large sign in the exhibit hall to "Take the Rubric Grading Challenge." While I failed the challenge and was not sent a free copy of the Rubric Converter™, I was urged to order one posthaste for one low price. Rubrics are lucrative in addition to being ubiquitous.

Rubrics' position as the latest sacred cow of writing assessment is no accident; rubrics make powerful promises. They promise to save time. They promise to boil a messy process down to four to six rows of nice, neat, organized little boxes. Who can resist their wiles? They seduce us with their appearance of simplicity and objectivity and then secure their place in our repertoire of assessment techniques with their claim to help us clarify our goals and guide students through the difficult and complex task of writing.

Yet, if you're anything like me, you have mixed feelings about rubrics. You've used them. In fact, sometimes you really like them. Still, you've picked up this book because something about rubrics violates your "deepest conviction about the complexities of the writing process" (Anson 1989) and you question your own use of rubrics: are they really all they're cracked up to be?

My own dilemma with rubrics crystallized when I taught a writing course at my district's alternative education school. Most students came to my class professing a profound dislike for writing. With lives complicated by varying combinations of poverty, pregnancy, drugs, probation, school failure, and refusal or inability to fit in, the safety of formulas and worksheets was strangely comforting; a complicated process such as writing left them confused and leery. But I didn't believe that students actually learned much or felt good about the time they spent filling out word searches. Knowing how important creative nonfiction writing had been to me, I created a Personal Narratives class and personally recruited (begged, pleaded, bribed) students to join.

When Felicity joined my Personal Narratives class as an eleventh grader she wrote about her grandfather's death. Felicity's writing was meaningful to her. She liked it, and it was organized clearly, beginning with a description of the moment she found out about her grandfather's death followed by her reflection on his life and connection to her. She used vivid details, relating a funny and illustrative story about a family tradition her grandfather had begun involving fishing poles, a song, and pennies thrown in a lake. The flashback was clear, the details relevant, the mechanics relatively error free. Felicity enjoyed writing it, and I enjoyed reading it. I graded Felicity's paper against the following rubric, which would be used by the State of Michigan to score my eleventh graders' writing ability on the MEAP (2005) later that year. I'd used this rubric before, and I'd never disagreed with anything in it.

Holistic Scorepoint Descriptions

Here is an explanation of what readers think about as they score your writing.

6 Writing is exceptionally engaging, clear, and focused. Ideas and content are thoroughly developed with relevant details and examples where appropriate. Organization and connections between ideas are well controlled, moving the reader smoothly and naturally through the text. The writer shows a mature command of language, including precise word choice that results in a compelling piece of writing. Tight control over language use and mastery of writing conventions contribute to the effect of the response.

5 The writing is engaging, clear, and focused. Ideas and content are well developed with relevant details and examples where appropriate. Organization and connections between ideas are controlled, moving the reader through the text. The writer shows a command of language, including precise word choice. The language is well controlled, and occasional lapses in writing conventions are hardly noticeable.

4 The writing is generally clear and focused. Ideas and content are developed with relevant details and examples where appropriate, although there may be some unevenness. The response is generally coherent, and its organization is functional. The writer's command of language, including word choice, supports meaning. Lapses in writing conventions are not distracting.

3 The writing is somewhat clear and focused. Ideas and content are developed with limited or partially successful use of examples and details. There may be evidence of an organizational structure, but it may be artificial or ineffective. Incomplete mastery over writing conventions and language use may interfere with meaning some of the time. Vocabulary may be basic.

2   The writing is only occasionally clear and focused. Ideas and content are underdeveloped. There may be little evidence of organizational structure. Vocabulary may be limited. Limited control over writing conventions may make the writing difficult to understand.

1   The writing is generally unclear and unfocused. Ideas and content are not developed or connected. There may be no noticeable organizational structure. Lack of control over writing conventions may make the writing difficult to understand.

Scoring Felicity's paper was relatively straightforward. While I felt that her "command of language, including word choice, supports meaning," and placed her in the 4 category, I gave her a 6 for ideas, which were "...thoroughly developed with relevant details and examples where appropriate." I wasn't sure if I was supposed to average the scores, but since everything thing else fell within the 5 range, I felt justified in authoritatively circling the 5.

Krystal, on the other hand, had confessed when she handed in her paper that she wasn't even sure what she was writing about; her piece involved thunderstorms, a trip to Texas, and a few tidbits about being teased by her cousins. The writing was a bit of a mess: full of inconsistent paragraphing, unintended fragments, unclear transitions, and spelling, punctuation, and sentence structure errors. I could tell that Krystal's paper was going to score badly on the MEAP rubric. But Krystal's paper moved me deeply, which I at first struggled to understand. I had read enough badly written student papers about traumatic events to know when my reaction to the disclosure was interfering with my assessment of the writing. But Krystal wasn't recalling a particularly traumatic event; her writing itself moved me.

I hesitated to circle the 2—a failing score as far as the State of Michigan was concerned. It sounded so harsh—*The writing is only occasionally clear and focused. Ideas and content are underdeveloped. There may be little evidence of organizational structure. Vocabulary may be limited. Limited control over writing conventions may make the writing difficult to understand.* But even if I bumped organization up to a 3, I could just as easily reduce the convention description to a 1—the grammar, spelling, and punctuation *did* make the writing difficult to understand, averaging out to an overall score of 2.

I fully appreciated Krystal's struggle with mechanics. Krystal did as well; she often approached me and asked me to help her with a word or sentence. I didn't want to dismiss the importance of mechanics to

Krystal's development as a writer; she needed to use words and structure sentences and paragraphs confidently and skillfully in order to better say what she thought. But if someone had asked me to hand over the best paper in the batch, I would have handed over Krystal's without hesitation. In fact, I had shared Krystal's writing with two colleagues and a friend earlier that day, telling them that *this* paper was what made being a writing teacher the best job in the world.

> When a thunder storm comes it gets as cold as winter
> The clouds turn gray
> Winds blows as hard as a tornado
> The birds stop cherping all the animals seem to disappear
> As if their being hunted by a wild animal
> You haer the thunder echo from so far away
> Seams clam then drastic at the same time sprinkles hit the ground
> The rain comes down harder and harder
> You hear the rain making a soft noise then it gets louder...
> Takes me back to a farm in Texas some time in April around Easter
> Where all my familee got together to celebrat...
> All I can remember is a flat surface of the horizon that seemed it
>   never ended
> Beyond was the biggest sun I have ever saw and the warmth seemed
>   so nice...
> I never liked the familie get together things
> because my cousins never really made us feel wanted
> Never made any conversation with my brother sister and I
> Maybe because we talked different I don't know
> But it seems every were I go I always some how feel missed place
> So when I think of sorrow
> It reminds me of a thunder storms
> Because of the colors gray and darkenss
> Because of the noises are loud and hectic
> The rain is like some one crying for an answer
> It reminds me of everything bad or sad that has happened to me
> I am thankful for everything because in away when any one makes
>   me feel missed place
> Or unwanted I don't let it get the beast of me because I feel like that
>   has happened to me a lot when I was a kid and know times have
>   to change for me and I need to stay strong
> So maybe that's why I think of my self as independent and I don't
>   think of myself as a follower or a leader and know I am happy

for who I am and it seems like no matter what the situation is I
always find away to keep my self conferrable...
After a thunder storm the rain stops the clouds are blue and the sun
is shining so bright and the birds start chirping and all the rain
has disappeared...

Even in its rough state, I found Krystal's writing more exciting
than many polished personal narratives I'd received when I taught
upper-level college prep writing classes at the traditional high school.
But nothing in the MEAP rubric reflected my excitement about
Krystal's paper.

Perhaps I was using the wrong rubric. Even though my students'
writing (and my teaching) would eventually be judged by this rubric, I
was not required by my department or district to use it in my classes. In
the interview for my teaching position three years earlier, I'd been asked
if I was familiar with the 6+1 Trait® rubric. The 6 Trait rubric had been
developed by a group of teachers led by Vicki Spandel in the 1980s and
she took a version of it with her when she went to Northwest Regional
Educational Laboratories (NWREL) in the early 1990s, where she was
joined by Ruth Culham. In the late 1990s, Spandel left NWREL. Under
the direction of Ruth Culham, NWREL added Presentation to the 6 Trait
rubric, and the 6+1 Trait® rubric was born. I'd never used this rubric, but
I'd been part of the NCTE listserv for several years and had followed several discussions about it. I'd even looked it up the night before the interview, and impressed at least myself when I'd rattled off the 6+1 Traits®:
voice, sentence fluency, presentation, conventions, ideas, word choice,
and organization. I liked the focus on voice; perhaps it would help me
reconcile how I felt about Krystal's writing with her score.

I found the rubric on the Northwest Regional Educational
Laboratories (2005) website. While I was shocked that it was fourteen
double-spaced pages long (weren't rubrics supposed to streamline the
response process?), I printed it. At first, I was hopeful. I could see that
Krystal's writing did meet many criteria for the highest score in voice,
including, "The writer takes a *risk* by the inclusion of personal details
that reveal the person behind the words," and "*Narrative* writing is
personal and engaging, and makes you think about the author's ideas
or point of view." Elsewhere, however, Krystal's paper scored worse
than it had according to the MEAP rubric. For ideas, her paper earned
the lowest score, because, "As yet, the paper has no clear sense of purpose or central theme. To extract meaning from the text, the reader
must make inferences based on sketchy or missing details." For organ-

ization, a score of 1 applied again, since, "The writing lacks a clear sense of direction. Ideas, details, or events seem strung together in a loose or random fashion; there is no identifiable internal structure."

Her performance on the sentence fluency and word choice traits fared no better; both scores were a 1 since "Sentences are *choppy, incomplete, rambling or awkward;* they need work. . . . There is little to *no "sentence sense"* present. . . . Problems with language *leave* the *reader wondering.* . . . Many of the *words* just *don't work* in this piece. . . . *Language is used incorrectly* making the message secondary to the misfires with the words. . . . *Limited vocabulary and/or misused parts of speech* seriously impair understanding."

But even with confirmation from two different rubrics, I couldn't bring myself to fail Krystal's paper. I wasn't even tempted to fudge a little bit and slide her by with a D. Did I want to give her an A? I wasn't sure, but I wanted to celebrate Krystal's writing, to read it to the class and say, "Wasn't that good?" to hang it on my wall and glance at it when I questioned whether I should stay in teaching or get that cosmetology license I'd always wanted. Mechanics aside, even the broad range of descriptive statements that the 6 +1 Trait® rubric provided didn't capture the essence of my reaction to Krystal's writing.

I reread the MEAP rubric to make sure I wasn't missing something; how could my reactions and the rubric be so out of sync? But, apparently, my reactions didn't matter much to the MEAP. As the first line reminded me, "Here is an explanation of what readers think about as they score your writing." Obviously, I hadn't thought about these things when I read Krystal's paper, and I began to feel that this seemingly simple explanation for the student was really a mandate and a warning to the scorer—*No matter what you really think, you will think about these things as you read and score this paper.* Well, I'm not overly fond of a mandate, so I put the rubrics aside to figure out my response as I read Krystal's paper.

I knew that Krystal's associative leaps—thunderstorms to Texas to language barriers to feeling misplaced—would confuse some readers, but I loved how her words hinted at something more. I could imagine Krystal's piece as poetry, and if I encouraged her to turn her writing into poetry, I wouldn't have to mark her down as much for sentence structure problems. But I thought that the writing worked well as a narrative. I loved the poetic quality of Sandra Cisneros' and Annie Dillard's prose, and I didn't think that associative writing and experimentation with sentence structure should be banned from narrative and relegated to poetry. While I imagined that some of the revision process for Krystal might involve elaborating, I also thought that part of the power of her piece hinged on its loose suggestive quality. Despite both rubrics' focus on explicit, easy transitions, I hoped that she chose to preserve much of the unconscious associative nature of her writing.

I also valued the exploration of context and marginalization I saw in Krystal's paper. While she didn't say it explicitly, Krystal's mention of feeling misplaced, difficulty with accents, the trip to Texas, and her connection to storms and the sun suggested her family's history as migrant workers. I also saw her many writing errors in the context of her displacement; she'd spent several months of many school years visiting her father in Ohio, so she'd not spent many complete grades at the same school. I'd spent a summer teaching English as a Second Language on an air-conditioned school bus with benches replaced by desks. We parked this roaming classroom at different migrant camps in the area every evening, and men and women who had just worked grueling fourteen-hour days picking carrots and asparagus boarded our makeshift school every evening to learn English. Some of these men and women had been professionals in Mexico; one had been an architect, another a lawyer, yet they earned more on Michigan's farms. Many of them told me that they worried about their children. Since they traveled from Michigan in the summers to Texas or Florida every winter to make ends meet, they wondered how their children would keep up in school. Krystal's personal story mirrored a larger societal context that I found important and intriguing. Krystal's story was not only important for her to write, but it was also important for us to read.

My appreciation of marginalization and the unconscious associative qualities I saw in Krystal's paper reminded me of my values as a reader of literature. I was fascinated by the texts and discussion I found in my postmodern literature courses in college. I fell in love with *Coming Through Slaughter* by Michael Ondaatje, a beautiful and unusual work of historical fiction based on the life of the jazz trumpeter, Buddy Bolden. At one point, Ondaatje injects a brief description of a woman cutting carrots. She cuts rapidly, caught in the repetitive movement of knife on carrot. However, the moment she thinks what she is doing, she loses control and cuts her finger. This passage has nothing to do with the plot of the story; the woman doesn't show up in any other section. I loved the initial confusion I had when I read this section; its lyricism kept my attention and I kept trying to figure out what it had to do with the story. My subsequent realization that this passage connected to a broader theme in the book—the allure and consequences of self-consciousness—felt like a victory. I'd solved some kind of puzzle as a reader, and felt proud of myself.

In addition, I valued the fact that Krystal was thinking through her writing. Felicity's paper was meaningful and interesting, but she didn't discover anything new by writing it. She knew before she started writing that she loved her grandfather and missed him, understandings that she put into words quite well. But she didn't surprise herself, or her reader, as she wrote. Krystal, on the other hand, stumbled onto some rather large insights as she wrote. While her description of thunderstorms was interesting in itself, she surprised herself and me as she began to connect the sound of the rain to her search for an answer and reliance on herself in the midst of uncertainty and rejection. Her writing brought both of us somewhere new. While Felicity's paper was clean and solid, I didn't see anywhere else for her to go with it. Krystal's paper was loaded with potential. I admired her risk and wanted to encourage and affirm it.

The MEAP and 6+1 Trait® rubrics failed to recognize my values as a reader and Krystal's strengths as a writer. If my assessment prompted Krystal to revise, the categories of the rubric would have suggested that she organize her paper in a way that would have changed the loose, poetic structure of what she had begun to do. I remembered how vehemently some of my classmates in college had hated postmodern literature; the leaps and associations confused, annoyed, or offended them. Apparently these same classmates had gone on to write rubrics. But if I created my own rubric to include categories such as, "Loose, associative leaps," "Explores issues of marginalization," or "Potential," I would have been imposing my readerly preference on Felicity's paper. Felicity's way of being in the world and thought patterns are much different than mine or Krystal's, and asking her to write in a postmodern style wouldn't fit the experiences and ideas she wanted to express.

What was I to do? The problem must be me—I was tempted to take a Valium and think as MEAP instructed me to think, circling a score of 2 with the authority of the State of Michigan behind me. Who was I to contradict the rubric? After all, I'd spent a lifetime immersed in, assessed by, and preparing to use rubrics. But despite all of this, here I was, stuck on Krystal's paper, questioning whether rubrics reflected what I knew about the complexities of the writing and responding process.

There Is a Cow in Our Classroom

How Rubrics Became Writing Assessment's Sacred Cow

In my teacher education program, graphic organizers were everything. Not sure how to teach brainstorming skills? Make a graphic organizer! Not sure how to activate prior knowledge? Make a graphic organizer! Not sure how students should begin the writing process? Have them make a graphic organizer! I was not immune from the craze, and impressed myself and undoubtedly my reading methods professor and classmates when I rendered the fragmented, sometimes nonsensical words, phrases, and punctuation in e. e. cummings' poem "Cricket" into a thoroughly clear and understandable chart. I'd never encountered graphic organizers in my high school or college literature or writing courses, but I had used them in science classes: to track the lifecycle of swimmer's itch or to wrap my mind around valence electrons or the structure of DNA. The emergence of graphic organizers in English methods courses seemed to herald the transformation of English classes into something as rigorous and legitimate as biology or chemistry classes—a transformation that seemed inevitable if the liberal arts were to withstand the pressures of funding cuts and accountability measures.

What were many rubrics, really, but ultimate graphic organizers—clearly defined performance levels organized into clearly defined boxes in a chart. While the Michigan Educational Assessment Program (MEAP) and 6+1 Trait® rubrics I'd used to examine Krystal and Felicity's writing were holistic rubrics—not designed to separate scores for organization or ideas—their language and structure were still clear and authoritative and they were ready to be transformed into a matrix by anyone with the table-making function on Microsoft Word or paper, pencil, and straightedge.

The rubric's association with graphic organizers and scientific categorization intimidated me and discouraged my urge to put the rubric aside when reading Krystal's writing. To compound the matter, the Northwest Regional Educational Laboratories website claimed that the 6+1 Trait® rubric was "the real thing," warning teachers not to accept versions without the registered symbol or to conduct 6+1 Trait® workshops without official training. After all, the rubric was "its most highly developed and tested version." And presumably required a "certified" technician to administer properly. Rubrics were apparently the next best thing, and my inclination to question them seemed to fly in the face of scientific progress itself.

I wondered how rubrics had achieved their elevated status in writing assessment—would their origins stand up under examination? I harbored a stubborn belief that the next best anything is the result of the best thinking by the best minds in any given field; my fascination with the "inside the factory" segments on Sesame Street where the marvel of thousands of perfectly shaped doughnuts dropping with breakneck speed onto miles of conveyer belt had convinced me of the efficiency of the systems around me. But I'd learned from history classes and painful personal experience to question that assumption: The products and processes of progress we assume to be the inevitable incarnations of human genius are often shaped by powerful and not always benign social and economic forces. I wondered if investigating the origins of rubrics would reveal murky beginnings and shed any light on my inability to reconcile what I knew about Krystal's writing with what the rubrics told me I should know.

To understand the forces that led to the creation and propagation of rubrics, I had to begin in a world without rubrics. To find this world, I had to find a world without high-stakes tests, a world where systems of writing assessment didn't exist because they weren't yet needed. To conjure up *this* world, I had to go back to the time before compulsory public education, to the beginning of the nineteenth century when less than 1 percent of the population attended public high schools in the United States, and only a small percentage of high school graduates went on to college. This time was difficult to imagine; I'd often warned my students of the economic implications of not going to college, let alone not finishing high school. Yet, in a largely agrarian society, knowledge was not as lucrative as it is today.

The scarcity of applicants in this preindustrial educational climate made a student's ability to pay more important than his academic performance. According to Mark Durm (1993) in "A History of Grading," "in the early years of Harvard, students...were listed according to the social position of their families (Eliot 1935)." Students who made it to universities were not necessarily rigorously tested when they were admitted or when they graduated. With universities and colleges desperate for applicants, admissions or graduation examinations were not tough, if they existed at all; a student's graduation from high school (and resulting assumption of wealth) often spoke for itself. The first college entrance examinations in the United States were oral. In *A Faithful Mirror*, Lazerson (2001) cites Harold Wechsler's description of these oral exams:

> a candidate would show up at the college a few days before classes begin with a letter attesting to his good character. . . . Faculty members then ask him to recite from specified chapters of Greek and Latin classics. All is over in less than an hour. . . . The student is admitted into the college proper, or into the school's preparatory department; few candidates are rejected outright since colleges are tuition-dependent. (383)

Education's obsession with ranking systems based on academic performance hadn't yet begun. Durm (1993) describes how, in 1871, Yale seniors elected a valedictorian rather than automatically nominating the top of the class as we do today. Letter grades and grade point averages were far from common, and while universities inevitably used some system to evaluate students, they experimented freely, switching between different numerical and descriptive systems every couple of years. Between 1851 and 1860, the University of Michigan used variations on a pass or fail system, a system that in the first several years distinguished only between those whose performance was acceptable and not acceptable, not concerning itself with the shades of achievement in between (Durm 1993, 3).

While no one would argue that education's elitist reliance on a student's wealth meets our democratic ideals, the absence of writing tests that ranked and sorted students by ability or achievement left writing assessment free to develop with the power of language and a student's progress in mind. Separate literature, speech, and composition courses, with their fractured emphases on decontextualized aspects of literacy, did not exist. Reading, speaking, and writing were simply a means to dialogue with professors, peers, and the community at large about matters of public interest. Drawing on the work of Michael Halloran, George Bohman, and Alexander Bain, Andrea Lunsford (1986) describes an integrated, language-rich environment that supported powerful literacy.

Classroom activity…was built around "oral disputation." One student chose and presented a thesis, often taken from reading or class discussion, and defended it against counterarguments offered by other students and the teacher. In addition, students regularly gave public speeches on matters of importance to society, in forums open to the entire college and the surrounding community. Reinforcing these curricular activities were the many student speaking societies where, as the University of Aberdeen's Alexander Bain was fond of pointing out, the students learned more from their peers than from their teachers (see, e.g., Potter 238–58)…this model of oral evaluation and the form of student speaking societies provided an audience, a full rhetorical context, and motivation for discourse, features woefully lacking in later "set" essays and written examinations. (3)

Lunsford goes on to explain how writing was part of the student's effort to understand and impact his society, as he often wrote out his ideas in preparation for his oral presentations. Assessment of these ideas was woven throughout each presentation, as professors, fellow students, and community members questioned and argued with the student, forcing him to refine his ideas and arguments—a process that inevitably strengthened future performance. Until the mid 1800s, writing assessment "brought all the language skills—reading, writing, and speaking—to bear on problems of public concern…[and] reflected a dynamic, collaborative learning model" (5).

This description struck me as an assessment utopia. I imagined the benefits to my students if this assessment model were followed today. Instead of receiving a static score from faceless evaluators after I sent her essay to the MEAP, Krystal might receive lengthy emails and phone calls about her essay that asked specific questions, made suggestions, argued, and praised certain sections. The point of this assessment would not be to rank Krystal's writing ability. Nor would it be used by the State of Michigan to determine her school's funding or to award or withhold Krystal's scholarship money or graduation endorsement. Rather, Krystal would use this assessment to become a better writer; assessment would be free to interact positively with learning since ranking her work was not its main objective.

But this assessment model didn't last long in the United States as the forces of industrialization and immigration created the need for a system of writing assessment that ranked students. Between 1820 and 1860, U.S. cities grew faster than at any other time (Caruano 1999), and the percentage of the population who attended public high schools rose steadily because schools were available there. As universities found that they could afford to turn up their noses at the rabble presenting themselves as ready for college, a new selection process was needed. The University of Michigan tried to solve the problem of admissions standards by certifying high schools, investigating a program and its instructors so that it would automatically admit any student who graduated from that school.

However, another group of universities led by Harvard began using written examinations in 1851 to weed through applicants (Lazerson 2001). These early examinations were not tests of writing ability, but tests of subject-area content that students would have accumulated throughout their high school experience. In the 1873–1874 school year, Harvard introduced its first test of writing, "a short composition, correct in spelling, punctuation, grammar and expression, the subject to be taken from such works of standard authors as shall be announced from time to time" (Applebee 1974, 30). As more and more students applied to postsecondary institutions, universities began to look for ways to rank these exams more efficiently.

The College Board had begun at the turn of the century to relieve the burden on individual schools to score and administer admissions tests. But like Harvard's early admissions tests, the Board's exams tested mainly curriculum-specific knowledge (Frisch-Kowalski 2003), and schools like Harvard complained along with Yale's Robert Corwin that the tests measured "what had been done rather than what could be done" (Hubin 1988, 58). Worried that Harvard and Yale weren't relying on its exams, The Board proposed a new kind of written examination in 1914 that set the stage for a growing focus on measuring writing ability rather than subject-specific content. Harvard had already established a "new plan" in 1911 to test a student's "power," or ability to reason rather than his curriculum-specific knowledge, and the College Board invited Harvard to reform its own tests to reflect this "new plan." The College Board's new written examinations were accepted by Ivy League schools (Hubin 1988), and the standardization of admissions tests took a giant leap forward.

Advocates of the "new plan"-type tests claimed that they measured mental "power." But the new examinations did not crack open the skull and let the observer watch the mind flex its muscle—it did not attach electrodes to the temple and measure a student's brain waves. The test relied on a student's ability to put thought into words on paper. As Hubin (1988) notes, Harvard's president Abbot Lawrence Lowell described the object of testing as "the ability to analyze a complex body of facts, to disentangle the essential factors, to grasp their meaning and perceive their relations to one another" (62–63). In this description, we see an echo of Vgotsky's description of the relationship between thought and word, of the process of expressing thought through language, of writing itself. The "new plan" written examinations along with Harvard's first test of writing ability in the 1870s helped set the stage for standardized assessments of writing ability.

While the tests' claim to measure mental "power" was undoubtedly an improvement over the rote memorization encouraged by previous tests, writing assessment was now firmly entrenched in a university's need to rank students. Universities' admissions policies have never been truly free from the urge to rank. Universities first unabashedly ranked a student's wealth and privilege then ranked a student's access to education as expressed through his exposure to a certain set of "facts" or curriculum-specific knowledge—which was another way of ranking his wealth and privilege. But in measuring and ranking mental power as expressed through writing, the new admissions tests unwittingly made writing skill the new object of its need to rank and sort. The relative freedom of the interplay among language, debate, and matters of public concern as described by Lunsford—and the assessments that were woven throughout this process—would begin to cave under the pressures of standardization.

As the efforts of the College Board attested, standardization was becoming crucial in the effort to rank students and their work or capabilities. The vocabulary of ranking includes variations on three words: *worst, average,* and *best.* Determining winners and losers, as everyone who has watched a contest of running ability knows, requires common starting and ending points and times. A man who crosses the finish line first but started the marathon three hours before other runners will not be declared the winner. The development of standardized measures for writing tests was less straightforward than for athletic contests, and had a predictably rocky start. Questions about the difficulty of the tests from year to year were raised, as well as questions about how to evaluate the writing samples in a standardized way. Dying were the days when the purpose of writing, reading, and speaking in colleges was to consider and work through issues of public concern; the effort to standardize writing tests and their scoring in the service of ranking would guide writing assessment through the birth of the rubric.

I'd initially been angry when I'd learned that the need for ranking and standardization was killing the "dynamic, collaborative learning model" described by Lunsford (1986, 5). But then I realized that in the world supporting this so-called utopia, Krystal was not likely to be involved in any dynamic collaborative learning model in the first place: her socioeconomic status and her gender were two strikes against her. And in fact, women's colleges had argued powerfully for standardized tests. If each student were judged by *educational ability*— not by wealth, not by gender, not by family connection—women's struggle for equality would make remarkable headway. The same argument bolstered the efforts of anyone not previously privy to the growing benefits of postsecondary education. Writing assessment's partnership with a university's need to rank students was both sullied by the impulse to exclude and redeemed by the desire to include: murky beginnings indeed.

But whatever their origins, written examinations and subsequent tests of writing itself thrust issues of writing assessment and standardization to center stage. As universities became more selective and the value of a college education increased, questions about writing assessment became urgent. If writing was now the tool by which students either succeeded or failed to be admitted to an increasingly important institution, how would the writing test be fairly graded and ranked? In addition, someone had to score all of these new writing exams, and professors found themselves staying late in the summer to pour through reams of essays from more and more applicants each year. How could the writing be quickly graded? In response to the growing focus on writing, Harvard created a new Composition Program in the 1890s, and the pool of qualified professors could not handle the demands of rapidly increasing numbers of students. The program began using overburdened and underpaid assistants to teach composition classes (Anson 1989). Without experienced, qualified composition instructors, how could the writing be easily graded?

At the turn of the century, Adams Sherman Hill set the course for writing assessment for the next five decades. Hill, Harvard Professor of Rhetoric and Oratory, was annoyed by the increase in incorrect English usage he saw in new students. He created and then distributed an "English Composition Card," which was a list of standardized abbreviations focusing almost exclusively on surface errors to the eleven instructors in his charge who were in turn responsible for the writing development of 630 freshmen (Anson 1989). Hill's focus on grammatical errors was grounded in tradition; English studies had long been overshadowed by classical language studies, and as English composition courses became necessary, they gained legitimacy by mimicking the methods of classical language studies: the study of grammar. As Arthur Applebee put it, "The shift of grammatical studies from the classics to English involved a shift from a method of teaching a foreign language to one of *correcting* a native one" (Applebee 1974, 6–7).

With one broad stroke, Hill's English Composition Card answered the three urgent questions in writing assessment: how does one assess and rank students' writing fairly, quickly, and easily? The card seemed fair because the corrections it promoted were nonobjectionable and applied to all. The card left no room for quibbling with messy and controversial issues such as content, context, personality, style, voice, or other matters that might cloud an instructor's mind: a misspelling is a misspelling; a fragment is a fragment. The card was quick and easy; the standardization allowed the instructor to bypass the lengthy and mind-bending process of thinking about how to respond to the writing, while the abbreviations made quick work of the response. As much as we might know better—good writing is not simply grammatically correct—the dilemmas facing Hill's instructors are eerily familiar: too many papers and too little time. We can both condemn and understand Hill's English Composition Card; some of us might even use his abbreviated notations such as "K" for "awkward sentence" today.

Hill's focus on mechanics and testing's obsession with ranking and standardization set up writing assessment to accept the multiple-choice grammar test as the next best thing. The military's progress during World War I in marrying the multiple-choice format with intelligence testing would prove irresistible. Like universities, the military was growing rapidly with the demands of a great war and was looking for an admissions test that would identify mental "power" in order to find leaders from among the commoners. Robert Yerkes, professor at Harvard and president of the American Psychological Association, was hired by the military around 1920 to develop and administer an intelligence test to all of its recruits. Yerkes used a multiple-choice format, created by Arthur Otis in 1915. Yerke's creation, the Army Alpha test, was the first large-scale multiple-choice test to be administered, and its publicity and popularity would pave the way for the same technology to be used by writing assessment.

The multiple-choice format served the demands of standardization and ranking beautifully, allowing anyone anywhere to score the same test in exactly the same way in a short amount of time. Another bonus of the multiple-choice format was that the results of the test could be quickly grouped, categorized, and analyzed in a number of ways; individual test-takers *and* groups of people could be ranked, sorted, and analyzed. In association with The National Academy of Sciences, Yerkes analyzed the results of the Army Alpha test, announcing that native-born American whites had scored highest on the test and that of all the immigrant groups, those born in southeastern Europe scored lowest. Carl Brigham, who had worked as Yerkes' assistant to develop the Army Alpha Test, did his own analysis, concluding that " 'selective breeding' would purify and preserve the intelligence of Americans" (Caruano 1999, 12). Added to the growing anti-immigrant backlash, Yerkes' announcement and Brigham's conclusions led to the National Origins Act of 1924, which established quotas for all immigrants to the United States. The most severe restrictions applied to no other group than eastern and southern Europeans—those who had scored lowest on the Army Alpha test. Multiple-choice testing had become a powerful tool of discrimination.

Writing assessment was ready to latch onto the multiple-choice test craze. While Harvard's examinations at the turn of the century still asked students to actually write, A. S. Hill's English Composition Card had shifted the focus of writing assessment to grammar, which could be easily and efficiently measured by the multiple-choice test. Writing assessment took the next logical step. Why should students write and assessors read that writing—clearly lengthy tasks—when they could simply take and score a multiple-choice grammar test?

The ease of administering and scoring such tests, along with their aura of scientific infallibility, promised multiple-choice tests an unprecedented place in U.S. education, a place cemented by the invention of the Scranton machine several decades later, a place it still enjoys today. Secondary schools began using multiple-choice tests first to sort and track students by intellectual ability, then to test students in each subject. In 1926, the College Board asked Carl Brigham, advocate of selective breeding, to develop the multiple-choice SAT to help universities sort and rank the "scholastic aptitude" of its applicants. By the 1940s, no remnants of the direct writing test remained. Indirect writing assessment—or the use of means other than writing to measure writing ability, in this case, the multiple-choice grammar test—became the name of the game.

Could writing assessment go any lower? Asserting that a student couldn't write because she incorrectly answered a question about gerund clauses was akin to arguing (with chocolate and crumbs all over your face) that your grandmother couldn't really make the world's best chocolate chip cookies because she incorrectly identified

"D. None of the above." as the reason that her sweet treats were so light and airy instead of "B. Baking soda." Even if there were a clear connection between writing ability and performance on test of grammar, the tests negatively impacted instruction. Why ask students to write in writing classes when only their isolated grammar skills would be assessed? Something needed to be done.

Not all writing teachers had eagerly embraced A. S. Hill's method of assessing writing or the multiple-choice grammar test. As early as 1890, Hill's own colleague L. B. R. Briggs had complained about the lack of response that instructors gave to students' writing (Anson 1989). Later, many secondary teachers voiced strong opposition to multiple-choice achievement tests, arguing in part that the tests required rote memorization without encouraging true knowledge (Hubin 1988). With such concerns, certainly this was the time for writing teachers to jump into the fray to create more authentic forms of testing that would have led the story of writing assessment happily ever after into the sunset.

But Harvard's written examinations and subsequent tests of writing ability had evolved for the purpose of ranking students, establishing writing assessment to serve the needs of an institution rather than the needs of the student; all new attempts to develop assessment methods would be judged by their ability to rank students in a standardized fashion. Patricia Lynne (2004) describes how composition scales, lauded by many secondary teachers for their potential to bring direct writing assessment back into the classroom, died because they could not reliably rank students' writing for the purposes of standardized testing.

Composition scales, developed by Milo Hillegas in 1912, attempted to rank students' writing without attempting to describe or define what good writing was. A composition scale was simply a group of preranked papers or exemplars; teachers would compare their students' work to the papers on the scale, find the best match, and give the accompanying grade. But while compositions scales provided standardization in the sense that teachers who scored different papers would refer to the same exemplars, it did not help teachers to agree on a grade. If a standardized scoring tool does not produce the same score when different people use it, it is hardly a standard. Without meeting the demands of standardization, the composition scales could not claim to rank reliably, and could not be used for the purposes of standardized testing.

A composition scale or set of exemplars would not have helped me to grade Krystal's work. Exemplars still leave wide open the issue of *what* we are comparing. How would I find a model that compared to Krystal's work? Would I pick an essay with fifth-grade spelling? I doubted I would find an essay that captured Krystal's original thinking, potential, and associative nature. The models would be too narrow to capture or capitalize on Krystal's strengths. If she used the essay at the top of the scale to revise, it would undoubtedly change the nature of the essay she set out to write. In other words, composition scales would leave me with the same problem in responding to Krystal's work that rubrics had presented.

But the use of composition scales in standardized testing would have encouraged classroom teachers to ask students to actually write, and their failure to reliably rank helped ensure the absence of direct writing assessment for several decades. By mid-century, many colleges were complaining that students were coming to them with poor writing skills and they thought that bringing back some form of essay examinations would force secondary teachers to place more emphasis on writing and thereby improve applicants' writing skills (Ekstrom 1964). In 1960, the College Board introduced "The Writing Sample," a standardized essay prompt that would be sent to individual colleges for grading. While the impetus for The Writing Sample's creation came from educators, it was still viewed with skepticism by the testing community.

Many were concerned that since different readers regularly assigned different grades to the same essay, essay tests couldn't be reliable measures of the proficiency of a single essay, let alone a reliable measure of a student's writing ability. Six years earlier, Edith Huddleston had published a review of the reliability of grading English compositions and had confirmed "what everyone knows: that grading essays for writing ability, even under the most carefully controlled conditions, is extremely unreliable" (cited in Diederich, French, and Carlton 1961, 1).

Not to be deterred, noting the effort and $97,700 the College Board had spent over six years trying to create a fairly reliable General Composition Test, Educational Testing Services' Paul Diederich, John French, and Sydell Carlton headed the study that would pave the way for rubrics. Testing had become such a franchise that the College Board had established Educational Testing Services (ETS) to create, administer, study, and test the tests: just as reliability had governed the fate of composition scales, reliability played a leading role in every ETS study. Other studies of scoring reliability had worked something like this:

... every effort was made to bring about high agreement on the grades that were assigned. The readers would be assembled; they would discuss and agree to certain rules for grading students' responses to the particular essay topic; they would grade sample papers, discuss the results, and revise the rules to cover all contingencies. After three days of this they would start doing the grading that counted. (French 1962, 5)

The scores were then compared. If the readers assigned the same grades to the same essays, the results were deemed reliable. If the readers assigned many different grades to the same essays, the scores were unreliable. But Diederich and his colleagues at ETS already knew that scores of writing samples were unreliable; they wanted to find out why different readers scored papers differently. Instead of specially training the readers in their study, they wanted to see what the readers valued in student writing if left to their own devices.

In "Factors in Judgments of Writing Ability," Diederich, French, and Carlton (1961) explain how they gave three hundred student papers to fifty-three "distinguished readers" from various fields of study, and told them to sort the papers into nine piles, using whatever judgments they generally used when looking at a piece of writing. They expected these readers to arrive at different assessments of the three hundred papers, acknowledging that, "if their grades do not agree, it is not for lack of interest, knowledge, or sensitivity, but because competent readers with their diversity of background will genuinely differ in tastes and standards" (10). Despite this acknowledgment, the researchers were disturbed that 111 of the papers received eight of nine possible grades, and no paper received less than five different grades.

It is important to note again that the authors went to great lengths not to discredit their "distinguished readers." They clearly took the differences in their readings to be valid. But college admissions tests leave no room for valid ambiguity; ETS wanted to be sure that the tests allowed the right students in and kept the wrong students out. The subsequent course of ETS's study would, in effect, try to wipe out all the genuine differences in individual readings in the service of reliability, efficiency, and the institutional need to sort and rank.

If educated and distinguished readers gave a single essay eight of nine possible grades, why use essay tests in standardized testing? In the Diederich study, readers were asked to make comments on the essays along with sorting them into nine different grade piles. If Diederich grouped these comments according to common "schools of thought" and distilled these schools of thought into factors, perhaps future readers could be trained to use these factors in scoring essays. In this way, they could arrive at a scoring tool that would improve the reliability of direct writing assessments.

Diederich, French, and Carlton reported what their fifty-three readers valued in the writing samples, painstakingly categorizing their comments and boiling them down until they reached the following five essential factors of good writing.

1. *Ideas*: relevance, clarity, quantity, development, persuasiveness

2. *Form*: organization and analysis

3. *Flavor*: style, interest, sincerity

4. *Mechanics*: specific errors in punctuation, grammar, etc.

5. *Wording*: choice and arrangement of words

This list of factors itself wasn't shocking news when Diederich and his team published it. In fact, the General Composition Test of years earlier had used qualities not dissimilar from the new factors: "Mechanics, style, organization, content, and reasoning."

The major influence of Diederich, French, and Carlton's list of factors was the legitimacy it lent writing assessment through the careful scientific process by which the factors had been derived. Pages of dense charts with titles such as, "Fields of Readers Having Factor Loadings of .25 and Above," "Correlations with 'Consensus Scores,'" and "Plots of Factor Loadings Before and After Each Rotation" gave the impression that the authors had irrefutably extrapolated the essence of good writing, and if readers were only carefully trained in identifying those factors, writing scores would be reliable and indisputable. Don't these titles bring back flashes of those white lab coats and two-way mirrors?

However, if we look carefully at "Factors in Judgments of Writing Ability," we see a far murkier picture of the scientific process than the nice neat list of five factors would indicate. The authors themselves acknowledge the messiness of their task, warning us that "It was hard to make any sense of the factors at all, and one should not expect the sort of evidence for each interpretation that would stand up in court. With this general disclaimer, we shall proceed to make what sense we can" (28). In this disclaimer lies the crux of the problem with the study, its results, and the reliance of rubrics on the findings of the study. To create the clarity of a list of five factors, the researchers imposed their search for order on a complex and messy process, necessarily ignoring and cutting out elements that resisted their categories.

This search for order began with the selection of comments they used to distill into the factors. Since the fifty-three readers of three hundred papers had produced 15,900 papers with comments, the researchers set out to make sense by reducing "the mass of data" to 3,557 papers, leaving out comments made on 12,343 papers. Furthering the search for simplicity, the authors reported that, "When a comment was unclear or did not fall into any category, it was not tallied" (23). In addition, thirteen categories were omitted from consideration in the final list because they weren't cited often enough for consideration. Anyone who has ever complained that standardized writing tests encourage conformity or generic writing will be interested to note that among those "Omitted Minor Categories" are "Originality of Expression," "Humor," and "Presents Opposing Idea."

The authors' search for the clean categories of scientific thinking effectively stripped writing assessment of the complexity that breathes life into good writing. However, their reduction and categorization allowed for the consistent scoring necessary for ranking via standardization; if we all look at the same isolated aspects of a particular paper in the same way, we will produce the same score. This standardization of readers is central to the success of Diederich and his colleagues' work, and the MEAP rubric's warning expresses their legacy perfectly— *This is what readers will look at when they score your essay.*

Understanding how writing assessment's focus on ranking and standardization had grown out of a specific time period helped me to clarify a nagging confusion I'd felt about the purpose of writing assessment. Long before I'd read Krystal's paper, I'd felt uncomfortable with my sometimes conflicting roles as a dispenser of grades and a writing mentor, and I'd always used the terms *assessment, grading, evaluation,* and *response* interchangeably. I knew I wasn't alone in my confusion: my colleague Amy, a middle school writing teacher, explained her own ambivalence about writing assessment in this way:

> I would say that I'm definitely ambivalent about writing assessment. What I really most love about teaching writing to junior high students is the privilege of being able to watch students connect inwardly to their opinions and outwardly to an audience. I like watching them discover and clarify their thoughts and share those thoughts with their classmates.

Usually, at the beginning of a writing assignment, I spend quite a bit of time establishing the assignment itself—what we are working to accomplish. But for the most part, the students spend quite a bit of time writing, and that's when most of the teaching and learning happens. While they're writing, I literally wander around the classroom, saying things like, "You look like you're stuck," or "Will you read me part of what you're writing?" I don't ask them if they need help because usually the kids who need the most won't ask. I'm interacting with them constantly about their writing. I'm watching and noticing things.

By the time it is my turn to put my hands on their paper, the grade is an after-thought. I grade the papers for the administration, for the parents, and for the few kids who are truly motivated by grades. In fact, for the majority of students—the kids who see themselves as B, C, D, or F students—the grades get in the way of their learning. Putting the grades on the paper isn't what I like or value about teaching writing. It's the interaction and learning I enjoy, not the grading.

Amy's description of her teaching practice shows the separation she has made in her mind between assessment and what she does to help students write better. She equates grading, which she finds to be of limited value in helping students write, with assessment.

We take ranking for granted as an integral part of writing assessment, but if wealth, privilege, immigration, discrimination, and the forces of a great war had interacted differently, we would not necessarily equate the two. We might see that all of Amy's interactions with her students about their writing are, in fact, assessments that help her students to become aware how their choices during the writing process impact their written products. But writing assessment's single-minded quest for the standardization that would allow it to rank students makes Amy's confusion with assessment inevitable.

Our understanding of the history of writing assessment can better frame our ambivalence and confusion about what writing assessment is and can be. But even if our confusion is understandable, Brian Huot (2002b), assessment scholar, suggests that "our inability to distinguish among testing, grading, and assessing or evaluating is one of the main reasons that teachers and students have misunderstood and devalued the pedagogical important of writing evaluation" (167). He claims that this misunderstanding has allowed writing assessment to be formed and articulated by everyone but teachers.

Assessment and composition scholars such as Steven Tchudi have tried to help teachers to sort through the terms associated with assessment. For example, in *Alternatives to Grading Student Writing*, Tchudi (1997) outlines a schematic designed to show how institutional pressures go against a teacher's impulse and research in grading. The first half of the schematic (see below in Figure 2–1) differentiates between response, assessment, evaluation, and grading.

Response

Naturalistic
Multidimensional
Audience centered
Individualized
Richly descriptive
Uncalculated

Assessment

Multidimensional
Descriptive/analytic
Authentic
Problem solving
Here-and-now
Contextualized criteria
Evolving criteria
Formative/process-oriented

Evaluation

Semidimensional
Judgmental
External criteria
Descriptive/analytic
Rank ordering
Future directed
Standardized
Summative

Grading

One-dimensional
Rewards/punishments
Rank ordering
Not descriptive
A priori criteria
Future directed
One-symbol summative

Institutional Pressures

Figure 2–1 Adapted from Tchudi's Alternatives to Grading Student Writing *(1997).*

This schematic is helpful in letting us know that ranking is not the only means at our disposal for responding to and teaching writing. In fact, Tchudi would advocate that we grade and evaluate less often and assess and respond more. But while the chart is helpful in showing that ranking is not our only assessment option, the placement of all of these terms on the same continuum implies that they are all more or less helpful parts of the same process. In other words, while we might not like to grade or evaluate because we don't find these processes helpful, the placement of terms on Tchudi's schematic implies that they are natural extensions of how we might look at and judge writing.

Our familiarity with Bloom's Taxonomy reinforces our confusion of assessment terms and encourages us to view Tchudi's discouragement to grade and evaluate with suspicion. In Bloom's Taxonomy, evaluation is linked with ranking (and thus with grading) and placed at the highest level of thought processes. Evaluation's linkage with ranking and position of honor in Bloom's Taxonomy suggest that teachers who hate grading view writing assessment as less than rigorous; they must be touchy-feely and soft on students.

But the history of writing assessment suggests otherwise and can help us to untangle our terms and reclaim assessment for our own purposes. Ranking and grading are not just our least favorite parts of the assessment continuum; they belong on a different continuum altogether because they have different goals than our goals as teachers. Writing assessment became linked with ranking to allow certain students into universities and to keep other students out. If we reject the university's uses of ranking students for our purposes as teachers, we can reject the legitimacy of these concepts to determine the current and future shape of writing assessment.

But rejecting one influence on assessment wasn't the same as defining assessment clearly. What did I think writing assessment should be? What ideas about assessment would I use to judge the rubric's suitability as the Sacred Cow or to look at Krystal's paper? I wasn't sure, and it would take more investigation into the nature of writing and assessment theory—and their application in my classroom—to find out.

The Broken 3 Promises of Rubrics

So, the rubric's sordid history was exposed. I was surprised by how discrimination against immigrants was mixed up in the history of writing assessment, and found it interesting that Krystal, whose family had immigrated from Mexico, should write the paper that precipitated my crisis with rubrics. But the case against rubrics wasn't cinched in my mind by any means. After all, many useful inventions don't have idyllic beginnings; just think of the treadmill, which was invented as a torture machine for prisoners. And despite the murky beginnings of rubrics, I could see the benefit to my own students of Diederich and his colleagues' work. As Bob Broad (2003) points out,

> rubrics may have done more good for writing assessment and the teaching of writing than any other concept or technology. During a time when educators were under constant pressure to judge "writing" ability using multiple-choice tests of grammar knowledge, the work of Diederich, French, and Carlton . . . legitimized direct assessment of writing (assessment that took actual writing as the object of judgment). (8)

Without the groundwork for rubrics that these researchers had laid, I would be busy prepping Krystal for multiple-choice grammar tests; my inability to reconcile my reaction to her writing with the MEAP rubric was a relatively good problem to have.

If I were to slaughter the Sacred Cow rather than simply chastise it for its illegitimate origins, I would have to examine all of the promises that rubrics make to teachers, promises that only the most stoic among us could resist: the promise to save time, to provide an objective grading tool, and to keep our teaching and feedback focused on the most important aspects of good writing. If all these claims were true, I should be celebrating rubrics instead of questioning them. However, if these claims didn't hold up under examination, it would be time to let the rubric go.

Assessing and grading student writing is an important job, a task that threatens to take over our lives if we don't keep our perfectionism in check. My colleague Keith is famous for taking an honorable but perverse pride in showing up at five o'clock in the morning to attack the pile of papers that somehow still spills across his desk year-round. Another colleague Dale recently underwent surgery to repair a tendon strained from twenty years of responding prolifically and thoughtfully to student papers. We all know someone like Keith and Dale, and we are awed and frightened by their efforts. We suspect that student papers may very well do us in.

When I was in high school, my English teachers had one more preparation period than other teachers because administrators recognized the enormous burden rotating sets of one hundred or more student papers created. With increasing pressures on school budgets, such allowances are all but obsolete. Within the past three years, my preparation time has shrunk from a daily average of eighty-two to sixty-five minutes at the same time that my teaching responsibilities have risen from ten to twelve courses a year—an extra twelve minutes a day that is sure to help me leave no child behind.

Rubrics save us time as they anticipate the most important criticisms and praise of student work, streamlining the response process. With a rubric, it was entirely possible for me to tell Felicity without writing a single word that her examples were relevant and that her command of language needed a bit of work. But an assessment tool's promise to save time, in and of itself, is never fully convincing. Tossing a dart onto a brightly colored dartboard with a bull's-eye labeled "A+" and an outer ring labeled "F" would certainly save time and perhaps even relieve stress, but we reject it outright (in all but our weakest moments) because it doesn't reflect any other value we might hold about assessment, including fairness, validity, or reflection of a student's efforts. The move away from the multiple-choice grammar test as an assessment of writing ability more realistically illustrates this point; even though it saved teachers and testing companies time, it damaged classroom practice as it discouraged focus on writing itself and misrepresented students' writing skills. An assessment method must convince us that it reflects our values about teaching writing before it seduces us with its claim to save us time.

Any attempt to compare our values about writing with the values implicit in rubrics cracks open the lid of Composition's Pandora's Box—our attempt to codify our assessment of student papers in numbers. While we may have found other uses for the rubric, such as developing a common language for writing, the main goal of the rubric is to produce a grade by articulating various levels of performance through numbers—the same goal Diederich and his ETS team had for developing the precursor to the rubric for use in standardized testing in 1961. Think of the various performance levels for "Sentence Fluency" delineated in the 6+1 Trait® rubric:

♦ [5] Sentences are constructed in a way that underscores and enhances meaning.

♦ [3] Although sentences may not seem artfully crafted or musical, *they get the job done in a routine fashion.*

♦ [1] Sentences are *choppy, incomplete, rambling, or awkward; they need work. Phrasing does not sound natural.* The patterns may create a sing-song rhythm, or a chop-chop cadence that lulls the reader to sleep. (Northwest Regional Educational Laboratory 2005)

Besides wondering how we would grade Hemingway on a rubric that defines poor sentence fluency as a "sing-song rhythm" that "lulls the reader to sleep," we could argue that any reader worth her weight in salt is able to tell a writer about the effects of sentence structure without referring to these performance levels. My students once told me that the sentences I wrote explaining an assignment were too long to be clear; without any training in the six traits, they understood issues of sentence fluency. This list of traits exists not because we need help identifying or articulating levels of sentence fluency, but so that we know what number the student has "earned" for their performance.

The rubric's attempt to codify our reaction to text in number goes counter to every instinct we have about reading and response. Imagine how quickly the conversation in a book club would be cut short if our meetings revolved around representing our responses to the latest best-seller in numbers: *Poisonwood Bible*—voice, 5; organization, 3. We might introduce these rankings as an inside English teacher joke, but the numbers would never be the focus of our time together; peeling back the layers in the text and the pure pleasure of the words experienced together would keep us coming back for more.

In addition, our experience as students of literature does not prepare us to reduce our readings to rankings or numbers. We may have privately and light-heartedly ranked the books we read in university literature courses, perhaps even made those rankings the object of friendly sparring with classmates. We may have written and distributed our own Top Ten lists or sworn that *Naked Lunch* doesn't qualify as literature, but our readings and responses revolved around the search for meaning in the texts we studied. It is unthinkable that the pinnacle of our study of *To the Lighthouse* would be a number; we would completely miss the texture and nuance of Woolf's ideas and how these are mirrored in her sweeping voice and narrative.

When our purpose in reading student work is to defend a grade, we do not apply any of our natural responses to text. Encouraged by the performance levels on the rubric to rank students against an external standard, our readings of student work are based firmly in a deficit model. We look for mistakes, inconsistencies, and unclear thinking to justify which square in the matrix we will circle. Bruce Lawson and Susan Ryan write,

> When teachers read student papers, they inevitably read against the grain...by approaching student writing with a skepticism quite unlike their approach to most other texts. (Lawson, Ryan, and Winterowd 1989)

The consequences of this skepticism are great. In our search for mistakes, we often miss potential. We should never assume that student papers will be perfect; our job is to help students realize what they cannot yet do. This involves a subtle but important shift in our view of the texts they create. It means that we articulate for them what they have succeeded in doing, explore the meaning in what they have written, and help them connect what is not yet there to what could be there. Created to numerically rank students' writing skill so that universities could figure out who could or could not enter their hallowed gates, rubrics have crept into our everyday practice. While we may concede a university's need for a gatekeeper given limited resources, our job as secondary teachers is to help every student improve, a role at odds with the rubric's intended role as a sorting machine.

Perhaps, if the rubric is only appropriate for evaluation at the end of the writing process—after generous opportunities for thoughtful feedback, readerly responses, and revision—we can avoid the pitfalls of rubrics by using them only for final drafts or even end-of-course portfolios. After all, we have to produce a grade at the end of the day. However, I was not alone in my frustration to reconcile the rubric with what I knew about Krystal's writing; the frequent inability of rubrics to express what we know about writing suggests that rubrics are not even fit for the task of ranking and sorting. My roommate at a recent NCTE conference recounts this incident during a session that she attended.

> In the middle of the discussion, a young teacher stood up and mentioned an essay she'd recently graded low because of the rubric she was using. With a truly pained look on her face, she kept repeating, "But the paper was SUPER. It was SUPER, just SUPER." She was still thinking about it, even though it had happened months ago.

Lind Williams (2005a), a high school writing teacher in charge of his district's common writing assessment program, explains it another way.

> My own district conducts a whole-district K–12 writing assessment using a six-trait rubric for evaluation. . . . [There is always a] very creative kid who refuses to be restrained and will ignore the prompt or rubric entirely (even at the risk of failing the assessment) . . . I read one of the papers last year and I agreed with every word the kid said, but following scoring guidelines from the district, the kid got a "no score" for ignoring the prompt and launching off on his own topic. Pretty engaged writing though, you'd have to admit. (2005a)

Writing teachers are not alone in their struggle to match what they know about good writing with rubrics. As writing-across-the-curriculum efforts spread rubrics to other subject area writing and projects, teachers in all content areas struggle with the limitations of rubrics. Kristi Zimmerman, a government, sociology, and psychology teacher, has been using rubrics since her second year of teaching. When she asked her principal for help with assessment,

> [m]y principal whipped out this matrix, filled in all the squares, told me it was a rubric, and said I should use it. I've used rubrics ever since. Of course, since then I've sat through writing across the curriculum sessions where I've been trained to use the things. But there have been countless times over the years when I'm grading a project or piece of writing, and I'll look at this really stunning piece, and then I'll look at the rubric, and if I do what the rubric tells me to do, the student will get a bad grade. So I'll admit, I'll find a way to add points somewhere—to get her to the grade she should be earning. Maybe it is some fluke in my rubric, but it makes me wonder if I am really limiting

kids—only the really brave kids go against the rubric. If most kids are using the rubric as a kind of checklist, which they do, then not only does my rubric produce incorrect grades, but maybe it doesn't promote or unleash what kids can do. (2005)

Kristi reworks her rubrics constantly, looking for the right combination of elements to match her expectations and her students' capabilities. But perhaps, as Lind suggests, "We keep revising our rubrics, but so far it hasn't occurred to us that it's not the wording of the rubric, but the very nature of a rubric, that is the problem" (2005b, 6).

Exploring why rubrics sometimes miss the mark when we apply them to our students' writing is critical not only for understanding the case against rubrics but also for grounding us in the complexities of the writing process as we begin to explore more promising practices. Essentially, any rubric with numbers attached to various performance levels is a mathematical formula or model that determines how different isolated factors of writing work together to create the effectiveness of a piece of writing; we plug in the numbers, and it spits out the grade. The grade's validity—or ability to reflect the "worth" of the paper—relies on the rubric's ability to predict how these factors work together to create good writing.

To understand how and why these predictions are often wrong— how a paper that scores high on isolated factors of good writing doesn't add up to good writing or vice versa—it is helpful to look at science's explanation of the way factors in mathematical models of systems add up to accurate predictions. This explanation starts with the idea that one event leads to another in a simple, causal manner—the idea of determinism. Determinism accurately represents the way that billiards games work. If I hit a billiard ball with a specific amount of force in a certain direction, it will move in a predictable way. The billiard table's controlled environment and the laws of physics and geometry interact the same way every time; thus, a software programmer can create a computer billiards game that acts very much like the real thing, minus pool sticks and too-tight Wranglers.

The rubric's grading mechanism depends on the laws of determinism, of simple linear cause and effect. Rubrics claim that if we just get the factors and weightings right, teachers can plug in the numbers and the rubric will reliably predict good or bad writing. However, writing may not be a simple system like billiards, subject to the laws of determinism. Writing may more closely resemble complex, chaotic systems like global weather, economic systems, or political unrest.

Science has found determinism inadequate for making reliable predictions about complex systems. Instead, the factors involved in complex systems work together in unpredictable ways. For instance, while isolated incidents of racial brutality happen far too often, not every incident results in the Los Angeles riots. Rodney King's beating was one factor in a complex, unstable system that exploded—understandably, but not predictably. In other words, if a similar incident happened today in your neighborhood, it may not result in anything resembling the Los Angeles riots. Factors in a complex system "swirl together" chaotically rather than build on each other in a linear, deterministic pattern of cause and effect.

It is hard to argue with Diederich and his colleagues that ideas are an important aspect of rhetorical effectiveness; it is difficult to disagree with Vicki Spandel (2005) that sentence fluency has a part to play in good writing. But it is fair to argue that these factors do not add up to good writing in any kind of deterministic, linear fashion. If writing is a complex system, it makes sense that Kristi cannot explain why her students' stunning papers don't do well on the rubric, or why the young teacher's SUPER paper or Krystal's writing got a low score. If isolated factors of good writing do not interact in simple and predictable ways, then the rubric does not mirror the complexity of good writing. Any numbers we run through this misguided model will fail to reflect our students' accomplishments accurately; whatever our view about the merits of grading, the rubric is not designed to do what it purports to do.

So, could I erase all of the numbers on the rubric, listen to my gut in giving Krystal a grade, and still rely on the rubric to streamline and direct my response to Krystal? All writing teachers grapple with what we value in student writing. We think we know it when we see it, but how do we articulate our knowing to students? The rubric attempts to articulate this knowing, and even when we give an overall impression grade, we rely on the rubric to provide a kind of working list of what good writing is: ideas, form, flavor, mechanics, and wording if we believe Diederich and his colleagues, or ideas, voice, organization, word choice, conventions, presentation, and sentence fluency if we believe Ruth Culham. If we create our own rubrics, we put many of these same ideas in different terms: content, structure, personality, or engagement. However we map it out, we believe that these lists keep us focused on what we value.

If we reject the rubric's grading claims and use them to direct our readings and put our reactions to writing into words, we must examine the rubric more closely as it shapes our voices as we respond to students' words. To examine this, we have to begin by acknowledging our con-flicted relationship with feedback and response. This conflict became clear to me when Chris, a student I hadn't taught in over a year, held out a handful of typewritten pages and asked if I would read them. I readily agreed, but wondered why: was this a scholarship application or per-sonal writing? Chris shook his head and told me that he'd already turned the paper in and gotten it back with a grade.

"Did you disagree with the grade?" I asked a bit warily; a favorite trick of students was to try to get as many teachers as possible to grade their essays as ammunition in their argument that they'd been cheated out of an A.

Chris shook his head again and blushed as he admitted that he'd gotten an A+ on the paper but there had been no comments on it. He said he'd worked for a really long time on it, and he liked it, but he wanted to know how to make it better. He said that he just wanted feedback, quickly adding that it was quite all right if I didn't have time.

Sure enough, I flipped through the pages, and there wasn't a sin-gle word written on the paper save the A+ scrawled in red at the bot-tom. I was immediately sympathetic: toward Chris, who hungered for meaningful response, and toward Chris's teacher, who was probably the victim of too little time and a confusing preponderance of teacherly conventional wisdom about responding to student work. In the previous two years, I'd sat through three inservices during which I'd been told that writing more on student papers doesn't do any good. One consultant had delivered this news with considerable glee: proof, he figured, that we'd been working too hard for nothing. He promised that if we picked one or two areas to "fix" in a student's paper and responded only to those areas, we'd save ourselves time and save the student confusion. He gave this response technique a snappy name—Focus Correction Areas, or FCAs. His proclamation and acronym had prompted a flurry of excited teacher whispering; some-one at my table mentioned that his students disregarded all written comments anyway and flipped straight to the grade at the back.

But this didn't match my own experience with writing and response. I wrote in middle and high school because I wanted to understand things and to be understood. I registered but quickly glossed over teachers' corrections, looking for comments about the substance of what I'd written: *Did it make sense? Did you understand? Did my writing move, bore, convince, disturb, or delight you? And why?* I didn't write for my teachers, and once took a bad grade rather than rewrite in a way that I felt would please the teacher but ruin what I was trying to do. But I hungered for meaningful response and looked for people to give it to me—my friend Sarah was an interested and thoughtful reader, and we often exchanged pieces of writing even though we were a grade apart. I couldn't understand how anyone could claim that students don't really want a response—unless their writing or the response wasn't meaningful to them.

The idea that less response is more stems from the view that the teacher's job in responding to student work is to fix errors. Donald Daiker (1989) tells us that as early as 1962, Francis Christenson identified this view of teacher response as the "school tradition," based on the idea that all change in language is evidence of decay and degeneration. If we remember Arthur Applebee's insight that the first English classes gained legitimacy by modeling themselves after the study of Latin, a dead language, then this view that our job is to fix errors makes sense; Latin is no longer a living breathing language, and we teach a version of it bound forever in time. If we allow student mistakes to stand, the language does deteriorate over time. When we transfer this approach to teaching a dead language to English, we are compelled to correct every student mistake; we cannot allow students and their mistakes to decay the language we love! But English, of course, is a living breathing language, and we teach versions of it that have been evolving since before Chaucer wrote of "that Aprill, with hir shores sote." Still, in 1982, Daiker confirmed that the school tradition was alive and well; he gave a student essay to his twenty-four colleagues at the University of Miami and asked them to mark the paper as if the essay had been submitted to them in a freshman English class. After analyzing their comments, Daiker reported that "89.4% of them cited errors or found fault" (Daiker 1989, 104). If we accept the school tradition's focus on correcting student errors and combine it with popular psychology's mantra that no one can take too much bad news, Focus Correction Areas make perfect sense: less response is more. However, no response is still simply no response.

Rubrics attempt to fix our confusion about responding to student papers in several ways. First, rubrics prevent teachers from turning less is more into nothing is more. Even if a teacher takes no time to write comments but uses the 6 +1 Trait® rubric and gives a score of 3 for sentence fluency, the student will know that "Although sentences may not seem artfully crafted or musical, *they get the job done in a routine fashion.*" In addition, rubrics prevent teachers from grading solely on surface errors. Surface errors are easy to find and we can justify grades quite easily with them, but rubrics direct us to honor other important

positive

aspects of writing. If we judge rubrics on their potential to help us move away from the school tradition of responding to student papers, they are a clear step forward.

But do rubrics help us to tell the truth about students' writing? Bob Broad (2003) acknowledges how helpful rubrics have been, but suggests that yesterday's step forward is sometimes today's step backward. Broad uses the striking metaphor of the Vinland Map to illustrate how our understanding of writing today is no longer reflected in rubrics. The map—simply a rough line drawing of the coastline of North America—is arguably the first map drawn of the continent by Vikings, centuries before Columbus' maps. Broad (ix–x) suggests that its simplicity was useful to the fifteenth-century mapmakers in their quest to determine the potential that this new frontier presented to the Roman Catholic Church because it told the mapmakers that,

1. There's land over there.

2. It's a very big piece of land, even bigger than Greenland.

3. It has a couple of big bays on the east side.

4. It's ours to claim.

Despite its benefit to Catholics in the fifteenth century, the Vinland Map is woefully inadequate for those of us who live in North America today. It will not indicate the general direction of Philadelphia from Michigan, it will not show which interstate highways would avoid traffic jams around major cities, and it will not indicate popular tourist attractions along the way. Broad suggests that rubrics have served a purpose akin to the Vinland Map. While rubrics sketched a rough terrain of the factors of writing that was helpful for early composition theorists and teachers, it is not a full or rich enough map for our use today. "After all," Broad points out, "we live here" (2003, x).

Even when used holistically, rubrics and their lists of factors are based in an understanding of good writing rooted in the infancy of the study of literature and composition. Every field of expression goes through a broadening of its own borders; the field of art two hundred years ago could never have accepted Jackson Pollack's splattered canvases or Rothko's subtle bands of color. Likewise, the study of English in the United States began with an extremely limited view of the form and content of good writing. Not surprising, of course, since early English studies had modeled itself after the study of Latin to gain legitimacy (Applebee 1974). Latin, a dead language, does not respond to the changing needs of a changing society with new writers who shape and reshape the language and its possibilities. Mirroring Latin's fixed canon, Harvard released a fixed list of authors whose work applicants would be expected to write about in 1874; all the authors were British (Hook 1979, 8).

Three-quarters of a century later, when the rubric was developed— after two world wars, the Great Depression, the newfound enfranchisement of women and African Americans, and an explosion of industry, technology, and immigration—a majority of educators still embraced this list and a myriad of similar lists that followed from Harvard and Yale—lists that included few if any contemporary writers who grappled with these emerging issues and circumstances. With so few models of writing deemed worthy of study or emulation, Diederich and his team's admittedly messy task of boiling down the comments of fifty-three esteemed readers was far easier than it might have been today. Not only were their methods reductive, but their esteemed readers also based their ideas about writing on limited models devoid of the complications of new ideas and forms of expression.

Since the birth of the rubric, the voices that have gained legitimacy— Whitman, Woolf, e. e. cummings, Bryson, Dillard, Morrison, Updike, Beatty, and Kundera, to name a few—have experimented with language, narrative structure, and modes of expression in ways that reflect experiences of life in the twenty and twenty-first centuries. These writers have changed forever our ideas about what literature can be. It is impossible to study e. e. cummings or Adrienne Rich and continue to think that Homer sets the only standard for poetic form and content. This broadening of our literary horizons should not be confused with a lack of rigor: Beanie Babies are not art, and my journal is not literature. The call for our assessment tools to recognize the broadening of composition's borders is not a call to loosen standards, but an effort to help students write in ways that reflect evolving notions of effective writing.

If rubrics, developed in the mid-twentieth century, are based on a limited notion of good writing, then we hold students to an outdated notion of good writing when we use them today. In a 1984 study by Sarah Freedman, students and professional writers were given the same writing prompt (cited in Huot 2002a). When their work was judged using a rubric, the professional writers scored lower than the students; the rubric did not honor the sophistication and variety of approaches that the professional writers brought to bear on the prompt. Since we use rubrics not only to judge but also to teach writing, our rubric-based assessment and instruction encourage conformity and an overly formal style (cited by Broad 2003, 4).

The disconnect between the writing we honor in our own literary lives and the writing we encourage from students is illustrated by our approach to teaching research and expository writing versus the research and expository writing we actually read. The *Atlantic Monthly* and the *New Yorker* include frequent examples of research and expository writing that draw heavily on personal experience and include use of first person. The recent *New York Times* bestseller *A Short History of Everything* by Bill Bryson traces the history of scientific understanding; it begins with the word *I* and recounts Bryson's experience and interest in large scientific questions. Even academic writing, supposedly the last bastion of depersonalized writing, now often includes and is grounded in personal experience. The word *I* in Bob Broad and Brian Huot's explorations of writing assessment theory show up in the first three paragraphs. Still, secondary teachers frequently invoke the "No I Rule" for all but personal narratives, poetry, and journal writing.

Limiting the kinds of writing that we teach and assess serves a purpose; it makes grading and assessment easier. If I overlay all my students' expository writing with my mental image of the model five-paragraph essay, I don't have to think twice before I decide whether their efforts stack up. I can easily give directions for improvement: this thesis sentence needs to go at the end or that general statement needs to go at the top of the funnel. Most disturbingly, I can even read papers without paying attention to writing's primary rhetorical purpose: how do these words affect the reader, in this case, how do they affect me? What does the paper make me think? What does it leave me to wonder? What do I want to know more about? How do the writer's choices contribute or take away from the way that these words interact with my thinking?

When we take ourselves out of the picture in this way—when we forget to let words affect us out of deference to a format that is easily identifiably and gradable—reading student papers becomes an unbearably dull exercise. I teach writing because I believe that students may have interesting things to say, and I enjoy the task of discovering, prodding, and pushing those ideas with students through language. I don't enjoy the monotony of checking stacks of multiple-choice tests using a template—which writing assessment becomes when we use formulas and the rubrics that support them. Rubrics direct me to read in a way that drains the meaning and joy from teaching writing.

The grounding of the rubric in early twentieth-century notions of good writing—based on the writing style of a few "masters"—not only encourages limited forms of writing and deadens teachers' ability to read for rhetorical purpose, but also taints our view of developing writing. Since rubrics honor the organization of a five-paragraph essay and we have clear examples of this format in our minds, we recognize the form implied in a badly written five-paragraph student essay, and we take comfort in that recognition. When we see an essay such as Krystal's that is organized differently than the five-paragraph essay, we judge it more harshly because we don't recognize its inherent (though incomplete) organizational logic. Not only do we score it more harshly, but we also provide feedback in a way that will only force the writer to rewrite in five-paragraph essay format. In this way, the standardization of the rubric produces standardized writers.

While our use of rubrics most obviously damages the student writers who refuse to fit into our molds, "good students" suffer under the reign of rubrics as well. Literature has broadened because the events of the last century could not be contained by the old forms; new ideas, conflicts, and discoveries have forced new vehicles for expression. When our teaching and assessment force students into a single mode of writing, we limit what they are able to explore and express through language. Those who conform to our molds may receive high grades, but we do not encourage them to develop the ideas and ways of thinking through writing that they may need to deal with the complex issues presented by today's society. Rubrics encourage us to read and our students to write on autopilot.

A common rebuttal to the argument that the field of composition has evolved but the teaching of writing has not sounds something like this: once students have learned the rules, they can break them; or, once students have mastered the five-paragraph essay, they can move on to more sophisticated modes of argument or expository writing; or, once students can tell a chronological story, they can play around with flashbacks and fragmenting a narrative. But my experience with developing writers doesn't bear this line of thinking out, and sounds suspiciously like the thinking that led a social worker to give my mother-in-law many desperate interventions to use when her infant son didn't seem interested in crawling and went straight to walking. My seven-year-old recently wrote a story that was full of attempts at flashback. Should he stop trying to use flashbacks until he has a twenty-year-old's capacity for accuracy in rendering sequential narrative? Should Krystal learn to write complete sentences consistently before I honor the effectiveness of many of her fragments and help her develop her poetic talents? When we try to "sequence" writing conventions or structures, or when we claim that students must master certain forms before they attempt others, we deny them the opportunity to develop those conventions or structures at the point they are most ready for productive interaction and instruction.

If the rubric's factors or traits are based on outdated and limited forms of writing, do we simply need to update our list of factors? Can we preserve the design of the rubric, substituting factors in line with more contemporary ideas about good writing? While Diederich and his colleagues developed their list over forty years ago, the 6+1 Trait® rubric was developed in the last twenty years by a group of writing teachers; shouldn't it more closely describe our values? Certainly, the consideration of voice in this rubric appealed to me in describing Krystal's writing. The mutation of the 6 Traits rubric into the 6+1 Trait® rubric implies the possibility of further shifts; if we add our own convictions about writing to the 6+1 Trait® list, shouldn't we have an adequate representation of our values?

But Broad contends that "a teacher [or a writing program] cannot provide an adequate account of his rhetorical values just by sitting down and reflecting on them" (2003, 3). Broad illustrates this assertion by spending a year listening to the conversations of trios of writing instructors and writing program administrators at "City University." Without the guidance of a rubric, these trios made placement decisions, talking and arguing about what they saw in student papers. Broad carefully recorded their insights and disagreements. He discovered that, "participants named a total of eighty-nine substantial and distinct kinds of criteria that informed their judgments of students' writing" (34).

I liked many of the categories I saw in Broad's criteria—texture, taking risks, shows promise, originality, and growth. These categories more closely reflected many of the things I responded to in Krystal's writing. Should we attempt to turn this list into the Broad Eighty-Nine Trait Rubric, register it, and proclaim it "the real thing"? There were several insurmountable problems with this proposition. First of all, I'd found the 6+1® Trait Rubric long at fourteen pages; even my rudimentary math skills were sufficient to warn me that if I extrapolated out this ratio, I would have a 178-page rubric on my hands—unwieldy at best and ridiculous at worst.

But more importantly, I shouldn't make Broad's list into a rubric because it came from a specific group of teachers in reaction to a specific group of student papers. And sometimes, we have no idea what we value until we run into it. I thought of a story my dance teacher told me about "Lamentations," a Martha Graham dance solo performed after World War I and at the beginning of the Great Depression. Ballet—with its upright torsos, limbs stretching to the heavens, and carefully executed poses designed to communicate nobility—had been the only legitimate language of dance in the Western world for centuries. Graham's audience would have expected variations on this vocabulary when she appeared on stage, sitting on a chair, dressed in a hooded black piece of fabric. Her contorted torso and arm movements looked nothing like what the audience would undoubtedly have said they valued in a dance. But much of the audience left in tears. Graham's new form of movement had communicated something about their postwar experiences that ballet couldn't. They could not have predicted their responses because they'd never seen this kind of dance; they discovered something about their values as she communicated grief through movement. The certainty of a fixed list enforces only the values of which we are conscious, dooming our unconscious values to repressed obscurity.

The reductive categories of rubrics don't honor the complexity of what we see in writing and what our students try to accomplish. Christenbury, Gere, and Sassi (2005) unwittingly acknowledge this with a strategy they call Thinking Backwards. Designed to help students better understand what scorers are looking for in standardized testing situations, the strategy asks students to consider a specific piece of writing and then develop the evaluation criterion for a rubric that would evaluate it "fairly." The authors reprint "My Name" by Sandra Cisneros from *House on Mango Street* and discuss how students can discover the criteria that make it effective.

> What rubric could be used to assess this piece? For instance, does "My Name" tell a fully developed narrative (no); does it use poetic language (absolutely); does it provide detail (yes); does it give us a full character sketch of Esperanza (yes and no). If we had to create a rubric that would fairly evaluate "My Name," what would it look like? (15)

The question is designed to help students think through what kind of writing different rubrics demand. But the suggestion that "My Name" might score poorly on a traditional rubric encourages us to create a rubric that will allow the writing to score well *because we all know the writing is good*. In this encouragement, I saw an answer to my dilemma with Krystal's writing: each piece of writing might demand an entirely different response, based on its structure, intent, and effect. In other words, we need to look to the piece of writing itself to suggest its own evaluative criteria.

We are accustomed to the idea that different genres might require their own rubrics. A rubric for an argumentative essay might include a factor related to counterarguments, while a narrative essay might ask for organization of events. But imagine asking Cisneros, Dickens, and Derrida to write different compositions within the same genre—a brief autobiographical sketch or a holiday update letter. We would certainly not expect them to write pieces that resembled each other in content or form. In fact, we may have asked them because we were excited by the different approaches they would bring to the same task. We might even expect to dislike one of the sketches. Short of using ridiculously vague criterion such as "Really Good Stuff," the Thinking Backward strategy and our own experience of these three writers suggest that to fairly describe the strengths of these works we would need three very different rubrics—rubrics that couldn't be developed until the writing was finished. And if we are going to the trouble to create three different rubrics, to respond individually to each piece of writing, what is the point of the rubric—designed to generalize, standardize, and streamline response? Perhaps we should take the hint that the authors of *Writing on Demand* didn't know they were giving and apply what we know about assessing established writers to student writers.

The Golden Rule
of Assessment

*Why We Don't Practice for Assessment
What We Preach for Pedagogy*

> *The process of response . . . is so fundamental to
> human interaction that when it is short-circuited,
> whether by accident or design, the result can hardly be
> interpreted as anything but a loss of humanity.*
>
> —CHRIS ANSON (1989, 1)

I was almost ready to turn the Sacred Cow of writing assessment into hamburger. But what would I use to replace it? I hadn't seen any acceptable methods of assessment in the annals of history. If the rubric was the best we had, why throw it away until there was an acceptable alternative? And how would I even know if I found an acceptable alternative? There had to be some general principles or values that would guide my search for more promising practices. At first, the only thing I could think of was the Golden Rule as it applied to assessment: assess others as you would be assessed. At first glance, the Golden Rule of Assessment is hardly a scathing indictment of the rubric. After all, there have been crueler and more unusual forms of writing assessment: the multiple-choice writing test, the sentence diagram from Grammar Hades.

But follow me, if you will, to a psychotherapy session. You are sitting on a psychologist's couch, relishing the deep, sweet-smelling leather cushions. You're pretty sure you aren't crazy, but you've been feeling rather flat lately. It could be worse, and you don't want pills to help you feel better, but you do want some clarity. You aren't usually a complainer, and maybe it's just the calm quiet of the room after a day spent managing the literacy of one hundred teenagers, but you find your story spilling out. First comes the pain of the present: your inexplicable tears, your difficulty waking up in the morning, your fear of failure, your paralyzing perfectionism tested every day by the chaos of your classroom, your argument with your mother last night about the Thanksgiving turkey. Then comes the past: your parents' high expectations, your sibling rivalry, your relationship with your mother. You are surprised by the vehemence of your emotions; you need a tissue. As you dab your nose, you notice the minute hand on the grandfather clock climbing toward the end of your session. You glance at your psychologist, who is taking notes in an official looking leather-bound notebook. Suddenly, you are acutely aware that you have told your deepest secrets to a near stranger. "What do you think, am I crazy or what?" you ask, laughing nervously.

Without a word, the psychologist tears off the sheet of paper on which she has been writing and hands it to you. (See Figure 4–1.)

"Your low score indicates that you need to keep coming back. Work on these areas for next time," she says in response to your puzzled look.

"But what about Thanksgiving? You know, how my mother wanted me to bake the turkey in foil and I wanted to use a plastic basting bag? What should I do?" you plead.

"Maybe you can answer that yourself after you've looked over the rubric closely," the therapist says smugly, ushering you to the door.

Client Assessment Rubric					
	1	2	3	4	5
Sadness	Feels sad most of the time.	Feels sad much of the time.	Feels sad sometimes.	Feels sad rarely.	Never feels sad.
Conflict with mother	Has overwhelming conflict with mother.	Has significant conflict with mother.	Has some conflict with mother.	Has little conflict with mother.	Has no conflict with mother.
Insight	Shows no insight into connection between past and present.	Shows little insight into connection between past and present.	Shows some insight into connection between past and present.	Shows good insight into connection between past and present.	Shows outstanding insight into connection between past and present.

Figure 4–1 Client Assessment Rubric

If you have any sense at all, you'll crumple up the Client Assessment Rubric. If you have any sense at all, you'll find a therapist who will ask you questions, someone who will help you understand what the Turkey Wars represent in your life, someone who will establish a challenging and invigorating conversation about your life in progress. You'll find someone who will respond with humanity to your humanity.

That your psychologist's rubric is a travesty but our writing rubrics are not is a testament to our acceptance of the artificiality of school. Schools often ask us to forget everything we know about the ways people learn, think, and create best. We know from experience that munching an apple or drinking a cup of coffee helps us to think, but food and drink are prohibited in many classrooms. We may read best lying down wrapped in our favorite quilt or with feet propped on the dining room table, but schools often insist on assigned seating in desks that would make most of us miserable. Our most brilliant insights might strike as we stare aimlessly out of the window, but we often close our classroom curtains or position students' desks away from the windows to discourage daydreaming. The very structure of school insidiously dulls our best instincts. Even the most idealistic teachers find themselves defending procedures they don't like because of the constraints of bells, four walls, handbooks of rules, and thirty students to a class.

In such a climate where what we know about human beings and learning is rarely honored, writing pedagogy has much to celebrate. Our view of our work is undergoing a remarkable shift: from the assumption that good writers are formed through listening to masterful lectures and diagramming plenty of sentences to the understanding that we must base our teaching practice on what real writers do—engage fully in the writing process. As noted authors such as Stephen King and Annie Dillard have published books about themselves as writers, writing teachers have taken note. The National Writing Project, which operates on the simple premise that it is difficult to teach something that you don't do, has done much to reinforce the notion that our awareness and experiences of the conditions, thinking, and processes that lead to good writing must manifest in our classrooms. In short, writing pedagogy is initiating a return to what we know about writing, thinking, and learning.

Based on this growing awareness of what real writers do, master teachers and authors such as Nancie Atwell, Ralph Fletcher, Harvey Daniels, Randy Bomer, and Lucy Calkins have advocated a workshop approach. Like working writers, students develop and choose their own topics, glean from writer's notebooks, write and write some more, revise, give and receive meaningful feedback, and publish. In 2002, Duke University acknowledged the influence of the writing process on its applicants' admissions essays; prospective students were told that since sharing, feedback, and revision were all important parts of the composing process, applicants should list the people who had helped with their essays and the nature of that help. While not all teachers use the workshop approach exclusively, many at least make time in class for brainstorming, feedback, and revision. Even when we give only lip service to the writing process while following more traditional methods we are part of this shift; it has become something that we know we are supposed to do.

Unfortunately, this shift in writing pedagogy has not translated into a shift in writing assessment. I played out my role in this divide between writing pedagogy and writing assessment perfectly in my first year as a writing teacher. I agonized over how to structure topic selection, prewriting, drafting, and revision activities in ways that were based on my own development as a working writer, and I often subjected my ideas and methods to the What Would Maja Do test: if I took my own class in an MFA program or as part of a writing workshop, would I demand my money back or throw rotten tomatoes? However, I never once applied the same kind of thinking to the rubrics I designed or the grades I gave students' papers. The truth is, if I applied WWMD to my own assessment techniques, my classroom would have been littered with refund requests and splattered with tomato juice. While writing pedagogy was based on reflection on what we know as writers, writing assessment was somehow immune from that reflection.

While we should not forgive my inconsistency, we can certainly understand it: this attitude extends beyond teachers, administrators, and testing companies. Pamela Moss (1994) remembers an article she cowrote in which she argued that standardized writing tests should include a teacher's written narrative. The teacher's narrative would give those who made high-stakes judgments of student writing context on which to base their decisions. When Moss submitted the article to a journal for review, the first reviewer gave it her "highest endorsement." The second reviewer recommended that the article not be published since a teacher's narrative would be subjective and perhaps unfairly sway the scorer.

The editor of the journal carefully read not only Moss' work, but also the two conflicting reviews. In the end, he agreed to publish the article if Moss and her coauthors could effectively deal with the concerns of the second reviewer. Moss points out the irony in the story:

the editor's decision took the conflicting reviews into account when assessing Moss' work, closely resembling the assessment process that Moss herself advocated for students. At the same time, by insisting that she respond to the second reviewer's accusation of subjectivity, he clung to the notion that fairness in assessing student work means objectivity as demonstrated by reader agreement and reliance on standardized measures. The journal's editor didn't preach what he practiced about assessing writing.

What is at the heart of this disconnect between pedagogy and assessment? Nancy Patterson (2005) tells a story that both illustrates this disconnect and points to an explanation for it. As the Reading/Language Arts Program Chair in the College of Education at a state-funded university, Patterson had agreed to help revise grade-level literacy expectations on which the state standardized testing machine is based. These expectations were due to roll out the following month to all state intermediate school districts. Looking at the writing assessments that were part of the document to be revised during the revision meeting, she asked, "What theories are underlying these assessments?" The revision leader, who had written the expectations and was the president of a statewide literacy organization, looked at her blankly, and asked her what she could possibly mean. After all, he said, these were *just* assessments.

This response reflects a common view that assessment doesn't have a theoretical base. We're slightly more familiar with the theories that underlie our teaching practice: writing workshops might be based in constructivism and spelling lists based in behaviorism. But assessments are *just* assessments. A meat thermometer is just a meat thermometer, meant to be quickly inserted and pulled out at the end of the cooking process; what really matters is the cut of meat, the marinade, the seasonings, the preparation process, and the temperature of the oven. An assessment just measures something, and isn't really anything in and of itself.

At first glance, such dismissal renders assessment impotent. If assessments are *just* assessments, they don't matter so much. What really matters is *how* we teach writing: our engagement of students, the effectiveness of our minilessons, our resolution of the Grammar Wars, our approach to teaching vocabulary, our facilitation of peer revision. We leave all that assessment stuff to Educational Testing Systems, the ACT, and assessment specialists who write our statewide testing programs. Teachers do what we do, and assessment people just take our temperature.

But we cannot afford to ignore the theories that underlie our assessments. The disconnect between writing pedagogy and assessment places us in a moment of great opportunity or danger; we will either push forward to redefine and redesign assessment to match our pedagogy, or our assessments will drag our pedagogy back to a place we have already begun to leave. Kathleen Blake Yancey (1999) describes three waves of writing assessment. The first was the era of objective tests, characterized by an emphasis on reliability and objectivity. In a positivist educational testing theory, reliability is the idea of agreement—that is, that a test is not reliable unless it produces the same results. A multiple-choice grammar test is reliable because two different people would score the test the same way. Reliability comes from an understandable push for fairness; before reliability, a college might admit a student based on his family name and inheritance. According to a view of fairness grounded in reliability, when two readers score the same piece of writing differently, the test is subjective. Objectivity and reliability go hand in hand.

The second wave of writing assessment still valued objectivity and reliability, but made room for validity. Validity tempers reliability—it is the idea that a test measures what it claims to measure. A spelling test is reliable because two scorers would agree on the right answers, but it is not a valid test of writing ability; perfect spelling does not a brilliant essay make. Rubrics and holistic scoring improved the reliability of direct writing assessment, which was seen as more valid than a multiple-choice grammar test. The increase in validity made up for the fact that essay tests are still less reliable than grammar tests. The third wave was the era of portfolio assessment, when concerns about validity, context, and interpretation began to override concerns about objectivity and reliability.

Yancey describes these waves of assessment as overlapping, which explains why we feel some backward pull of the first objective testing wave still. She suggests that in the overlap between other waves, teachers have called for a match between emerging paradigms of writing pedagogy and outdated forms of assessment.

> [T]eachers saw the difference between what they taught in their classes—writing—and what was evaluated—selection of homonyms and sentence completion exercises...they thought that difference mattered; and...they continued to address this disjunction rhetorically, as though the testing enterprise could be altered....Still it took over 20 years for this critique to make an impact, over 20 years for the second wave to occur. It's fair to ask, then: if compositionists saw

this disjunction between classroom practice and testing practice early on, why did it take over two decades to shift . . . from one methodology to another?" (486–487)

It is a question we might ask ourselves. With writing pedagogy's clear focus on process and what working writers do, what keeps our assessments from following suit?

Movement between the first three waves of writing assessment was relatively fluid compared to the present paralyzing pull between the past and future of writing assessment. Yancey suggests that we are in the era of portfolio assessment, but in the years since her article was published, the portfolio wave has failed to gain momentum, pulling back on itself (Lynne 2004). Portfolios, which give students time, choice, multiple samples, and the benefits of feedback and revision have been criticized for failing to demonstrate reliability. In addition, as states struggle to fund schools, many portfolio assessments have been dropped. Michigan's assessment program, which once allowed time for revision, sharing, feedback, reflective writing, and writing done in the classroom has progressively cut these so-called frills, and plans to bring back some form of the multiple-choice grammar test and sentence-combining exercises and will be outsourcing its testing duties to the ACT in 2006 to save money. In many classrooms, portfolios are simply a collection of independently scored essays, violating the reflective, dialectic nature of portfolios. Why do we seem to have lost ground?

Patricia Lynne (2004) suggests that we cannot move forward until writing assessment undergoes a paradigm shift between positivism and constructivism. She points out that Yancey describes movement between previous waves as shifting tensions between two terms: reliability and validity, allowing fairly easy movement between the three waves. If this is true, in economic funding crises, the least expensive balance between these terms will become acceptable—and since we have found the multiple-choice grammar test to be a relatively cheap and reliable test of writing ability, concerns about its validity defer to budget concerns. But these terms do not describe or support the ideas we have come to view as the basis of writing pedagogy, rendering even the most productive shift toward validity and away from reliability insufficient. Lynne reminds us that the terms *reliability, validity,* and *objectivity* are terms based firmly in positivism. She argues that positivism supports a technocratic paradigm that writing pedagogy has left behind in favor of constructivist and contextual paradigms (3–12). I find it helpful to look at the difference between the practices spawned by these different paradigms; this comparison not only helps me to understand Lynne's arguments, but also allows me to see my values and instincts about teaching in the context of larger ideas. (See Figure 4–2.)

Two Views of Literacy and How We Teach Them	
Technocratic Paradigm	**Constructivist and Contextual Paradigms**
Key terms and concepts: *functional literacy, skills, sequential learning, training, value neutral, part-whole*	Key terms and concepts: *context, construction of meaning, interpretation, disagreement, reader response, recursive, scaffolding*
The goal of literacy is to create workers who can read and write well enough to contribute in an industrial, capitalistic society. *Functional literacy, defined as the ability to read and write at a fifth-grade level, was considered to be the goal of public literacy education.*	The goal of literacy is to construct meaning from and through language. *The idea that teachers must "activate prior knowledge" is based on the idea that students must make meaning by connecting new learning to their own experiences.* *Reader response assumes that every text becomes slightly different in each reader's mind as they overlay the text with his or her own experiences.*
The whole must be separated into parts in order to be understood. *Phonics instruction breaks down the sounds of words into manageable chunks. Formulaic essay instruction (five-paragraph, Schaffer method) relies on the idea that teaching students how to write different parts of the essay well adds up to good writing.*	Understanding discrete parts does not necessarily lead to understanding of the whole; the whole is not simply the sum of its parts. *Phonics instruction must be part of a well-balanced, whole-language approach to reading and writing instruction.*
Language skills are sequential. *Graduated readers express the idea that one set of literacy skills need to be mastered before another is tackled.* *Articulated grade-level expectations are important to help teachers move students smoothly through progressive stages of literacy.*	Language skills are not sequential, but recursive. *Scaffolding operates on the idea that students don't master skills, but return to them with different levels of sophistication throughout their school experience.*
Meaning is fixed in texts and rules of grammar and composition. *Since the goal of literacy is to become a good worker, the goal of literacy is to follow instructions well.* *The intent of the author and the experiences of the reader have no bearing on the meaning of the text itself; meaning is derived from the technical properties and structure of language alone.*	The meaning we construct as writers and readers depends, in large part, on the contexts in which we find ourselves—our race, class, gender, politics, age, experiences, and position within or without power structures. *Multiple literacies are recognized: computer literacy, cultural literacy, ideological literacy.* *Literature studies recognize multiple lenses of interpretation: Marxist, feminist, etc.*

Figure 4–2 *Two Views of Literacy and How We Teach Them*

Lynne says that positivism fits well within the technocratic paradigm, but not within constructivism or a contextual paradigm. In a contextual paradigm, those positioned closest to students have the deepest understanding of their literacy contexts—an understanding critical for teaching and assessment. But positivism puts context in conflict with objectivity, dictating that student writing samples be sent to anonymous scorers rather than to the students' teachers—a teacher's knowledge of a student might skew scores. In addition, the demands of reliability clash with a constructivist's focus on multiple lenses of interpretation and disagreement. While constructivism would allow for and value many different readings of a student's writing, reliability demands that all readers read the same way and produce the same score. While constructivism would value the debate spawned by various interpretations, reliability would view this debate as a failure of agreement. In other words, the next wave of writing assessment is so long in coming because we must do more than shift emphasis between reliability and validity: we must change paradigms and the terms that accompany them altogether.

Lynne's argument explains why the wave of portfolio assessment seems to have slipped from beneath us. As long as reliability and objectivity define writing assessment, portfolios will always seem expensive, subjective, and bulky. Instead of scoring the whole portfolio, positivism's push for reliability breaks the portfolio into manageable, scoreable chunks—which means that scorers must score more than one essay for each student. Or, if scorers treat the portfolio as a whole, reliability requires scorers to spend more time norming themselves—looking at sample portfolios and making sure that they all give the same grade most of the time. Failure to break the portfolio into manageable chunks or to spend time norming readers precipitates a failure of reliability and objectivity, rendering portfolios either expensive and bulky or unreliable and subjective. The multiple samples generated by portfolios are not met with multiple interpretations and discussions, but with a mounting and expensive effort to create a single interpretation and score. No wonder positivism finds portfolios problematic! No wonder the portfolio wave of writing assessment has failed to crest and the riptide of objectivity and reliability are pulling us out to sea.

Not all composition theorists agree with Patricia Lynne. While assessment scholars such as Brian Huot or Pamela Moss might acknowledge problems with reliability and objectivity, they would argue that positivism has too much power to ignore altogether. Huot

(2002a) points out that the definition of validity is being pushed by scholars such as Messick and Cronbach to mean not only that a test measures what it says it measures, but also that the theory underlying the test must be recognizable and supportable. Huot finds hope for writing assessment in a shift within positivism.

But Lynne implies that investing in validity is not enough. "While there is much to celebrate in the theoretical changes in validity, reliability remains a key concept in educational measurement theory and thus remains a problem" (Lynne 2004, 76). This explains why Pamela Moss' editor criticized her call for bringing potentially conflicting teacher narratives of student work into the standardized testing conversation—this model violates reliability, even though the editor followed a review process that valued disagreement. Without a shift from positivism, writing assessment theory will never support the assessment practices on which working writers rely. We will either be forced to reject the writing process in favor of a writing pedagogy that can be efficiently and reliably assessed, or we will continue to operate with our assessments and our practice out of sync.

We have been told repeatedly in curriculum alignment task forces and assessment courses that our tests must match what we teach. We are warned not to become that college professor we once had whose midterm exam bore no resemblance to any material covered in the syllabus, lectures, or texts. We need to take this admonishment to its logical conclusion: our assessments should be based on the same assumptions as our pedagogy. If we accept the assumption that, as writing teachers, we should want for our students what we want for ourselves as writers, we should demand no less of our assessments.

While we leave emerging theories of and debate about writing assessment in Lynne's and Huot's capable hands for now—understanding that it may take many years for the measurement community to find the right match between our pedagogy and assessment—we are left with the question of what to do in our own classrooms. Our students may be forced for many years to express their writing ability through taking multiple-choice grammar tests, writing to generic prompts such as "Friends," and being assessed by equally generic rubrics. But Yancey's reminder that teachers have forced each new wave of writing assessment should give us resolve. We cannot build momentum for the next wave of writing assessment unless we start developing and doing in our classrooms what we wish our assessments to do. What kinds of assessment tools *do* we want for ourselves and for our students?

Agreeing to Disagree

The Heart of a New Writing Assessment Paradigm

My brother and I fought constantly and bitterly when we were growing up. We drew an imaginary line between ourselves in the small blue family Nova, sometimes buttressing it with stacks of books or sofa cushions. The violation of this line would spur a round of flailing elbows, knees, and insults that drove my poor parents to distraction. I once overheard my mother bemoaning our antics to her sister. "Conflict is good," my aunt told her. "They're practicing now for getting along later." Little consolation to my mother, of course, but my aunt's reply stunned me. Conflict could be productive?

The thought that there might be a motivation behind conflict that transcended pure meanness began to shape my experiences. I continued to wage The Elbow Wars with my brother for quite a few years, but I began to listen for the impulse beneath disagreements. I prided myself on finding middle ground and shaping conflicting views into new solutions. I gained confidence in voicing dissent; my desperate adolescent need to be liked couldn't outweigh my joy in a good argument. I developed a distrust for surfaces undisturbed by debate—who could agree all of the time and who would want to? My aunt's proclamation had begun to shift my understanding of conflict.

Our writing assessment paradigm for students is marked by a fear of disagreement. In standardized testing norming sessions, those raters who consistently score differently than the majority are dismissed. Our most trusty assessment tool—the rubric—was created to manufacture consensus. If we all focus similarly on the same qualities of writing, we will look at student papers the same way. When we distribute and teach the rubric throughout the writing process, we ensure that students agree with our assessments—we point to it when our judgments are questioned as if to say, "It isn't just *me* who thinks this. Disagree with me, and you're disagreeing with the rubric and the entire field of writing assessment." Who wants to be on the other side of *that* argument?

This fear of disagreement has profound existential roots. When I was in elementary school, I remember being transfixed by the question of how anyone could know if the blue I saw was the same blue that anyone else saw. Ultimately, I didn't know—an unknowing with the power to skew all of my perceptions. If I couldn't even know if we see the same blue, how could I really know someone else—what another person is feeling, thinking, or seeing? More importantly, how could anyone know me? To avoid feeling profoundly alone, I settled the question of how we know blue is blue with variations on, "Well, everyone says it is blue. We all agree." Agreement, then, saved me from struggling with the uncertainty of things I didn't know.

But agreement can also keep us from understanding. In communications theory, Irving Janis (1982) called this phenomenon *groupthink*, a process that takes over when members of a group are so motivated to agree that they dismiss ideas or paths of action that might cause conflict. Janis' work focused on groups that made decisions resulting in disastrous courses of action: The Bay of Pigs conflict; The Korean War; Pearl Harbor; and The Cuban Missile Crisis. His studies concluded that while groups need multiple perspectives to understand a complex problem, some groups are so driven to achieve consensus that they shut down disagreement in favor of simple solutions that do not acknowledge the vastness of the problem.

Later communications theorists began to apply Janis' ideas to smaller groups, arguing that groupthink can happen any time people set out to tackle a complex problem. We could argue that groupthink characterizes the push for agreement in writing assessment. The rubric—accompanied by norming sessions that encourage readers to come to the same reading and score of student work—is the formalized manifestation of groupthink. Rubrics enforce and perpetuate agreement in the field of writing assessment, making little room for the multiple perspectives, readings, and insights that would give us a better understanding of the complexities of the writing process.

A conversation I overheard earlier this year in a rubric norming session illustrates how rubrics encourage teachers to shut down disagreement in favor of agreement—to the detriment of real insight about writing. My county's intermediate school district was attempting to institute an English Language Arts (ELA) curriculum with anchor assignments and common rubrics for all county districts. Groups of teachers were gathered around tables, reading and discussing eighth-grade essays written to the common in-class writing prompt, "Friends." One paper was written by a young woman who wrote about how she met her boyfriend. In the essay, she revealed that she and her boyfriend enjoyed going to movies together. The ELA leader began the conversation by asking what general impressions teachers had of the paper. The ensuing conversation went something like this,

TEACHER 1: (*tentatively*) I didn't really like it.

LEADER: Why not?

TEACHER 1: Well, an eighth grader should be able to do better.

TEACHER 2: But it is decent writing.

TEACHER 1: I guess I wouldn't give this paper a good grade in one of my classes.

TEACHER 2: But what's wrong with it?

LEADER: Let's look at the rubric and see how this paper breaks down. What score did you give for organization?

TEACHER 2: It's organized. I gave it a 4.

TEACHER 3: I don't know—it's boring. I gave it a 1.

TEACHER 4: But boring and organization aren't the same.

TEACHER 2: Yeah, it's sequential. First one thing happens, then another, then another: she likes him; he asks her out; they go out. It's clear. It's organized.

TEACHER 3: But that sequential organization makes it boring. There is nothing going on in the paper. *I met my boyfriend. We went to a movie. He brought me flowers. He is my friend.*

TEACHER 1: Yeah, boyfriend papers should definitely be banned. (*Group laughs.*)

TEACHER 2: But it's still organized, so for organization it gets a 4. If we had a category for boring, maybe it would get a 1 there.

TEACHER 4: But we can't have a category for boring, can we? I mean, what is boring for you might not be boring for me. Although I really do think this is kind of boring.

TEACHER 3: But can't the organization of the paper either create the boredom or excitement of the paper? What if we'd had a flash-back of the student's fears about dating or loneliness in the middle of this paper? Part of the problem with this paper is that it is so surface—and if there were a flashback—well, maybe wouldn't it be more interesting? Wouldn't that kind of organization make it more interesting?

TEACHER 4: But the rubric doesn't say anything about that. It just wants to know if it is organized. It still earns a 4 because it is organized.

Conflict first occurs in the conversation between Teacher 1, who thinks eighth-grade students should be able to do better, and Teacher 2, who thinks that the paper is well written. Instead of exploring the attitudes and assumptions beneath these conflicting statements, the rubric-norming leader does her job: she directs the teachers to consult the rubric. The second conflict, between Teachers 3 and 4, revolves around whether the paper is interesting and whether this has anything to do with the organization of the paper. This conflict is solved by the rubric again the rubric does not care if the paper is boring. As Teacher 4 puts it, "...the rubric doesn't say anything about that."

In every conversation throughout this norming session, the most interesting lines of inquiry into students' work are shut down for the sake of agreement. The push for agreement centered on the rubric will also thwart conversations Teacher 4 might have with his student about how to make this paper better. Teacher 4 thinks that the paper is boring, but understands that the language on the rubric indicates he should give the paper the highest possible score for organization. Despite his concerns, what motivation does the teacher have to suggest that the student consider organizing the paper differently if he has earned a perfect organization score? The rubric overrides his reactions to writing.

It would be tempting to dismiss this criticism of agreement by condemning the particular rubric used in this session. If the wording of the rubric had incorporated some mention of engagement, Teacher 3's argument might have stood a chance. But it is important to pay attention to the how the rubric mediates the teachers' thoughts, responses, and negotiation of conflict—no matter how careful the wording. The rubric doesn't just focus teachers' attention; it demands deference. In fact, Teacher 4 personifies the rubric, referring to what the rubric "wants." The teachers rely on the rubric to solve their disagreements, shutting down potentially interesting discussions—their own insights about writing—because they don't appear on the rubric. But this is no surprise. This rush to agreement is the very mechanism by which the rubric works to increase the reliability of direct writing assessment. Lind Williams (2005a), high school English teacher and literacy specialist, reflects on how the rubric mediates conversations about writing in his district's assessment program.

> I think the best discussions about what makes good writing came up in the committee that designed the rubric because we basically started from scratch...once the rubric is written it's as if Moses has come down from the mountain. There is discussion about what the rubric means and how those qualities would look in a paper, but there is very little discussion about matters "beyond" the rubric.

Vicki Spandel (2005) advises teachers to make their own rubrics to avoid viewing any particular rubric as the Ten Commandments of Writing, but there are several problems with this advice. Developing our own rubrics undermines the standardization rubrics were created to provide. If we accept the suitability of rubrics for writing assessment, we implicitly accept the need for this standardization: why wouldn't we base our rubrics on state- and districtwide writing assessment program rubrics? After all, our success is judged by how well our students perform on these measures. And when we do create our own rubrics in practice, we don't deviate much from Diederich or Spandel's lists, frequently only adding assignment-specific factors such as "Addresses at least three counterarguments" or "Discusses Golding's use of symbol."

But even more important, developing our own rubrics doesn't change their reductive nature. As we've already seen Bob Broad argue, "...a teacher [or a writing program] cannot provide an adequate account of his rhetorical values just by sitting down and reflecting on them" (2003, 3). His work suggests that the reductive nature of rubrics makes them unsuitable for capturing what we value about writing, whether we create them or our state assessment programs create them. He writes,

> Theories of learning, composition, and writing assessment have evolved to the point at which the method and technology of the rubric now appear dramatically at odds with our . . . pedagogical . . . commitments. In short, traditional rubrics and scoring guides prevent us from telling the truth about what we believe, what we teach, and what we value in composition courses and programs. (2)

In our obsession with agreement, we have accepted a writing assessment tool that causes us to miss what our students are doing and to ignore what we really think. In contrast, our writing assessment paradigm for working writers allows for and is centered on the conflict and disagreement that erupt when very different people pay attention to their minds, hearts, and guts when reacting to writing. The virtue of conflict in the publishing world begins with editors who are willing to disagree with their colleagues' assessment of writing, discovering some of the most interesting writers along the way. Jack Prelutsky, an author of children's books of poetry, was rejected by legendary editor Ursula Nordstrom before meeting Susan Hirschman at Macmillan Books. Prelutsky gave Hirschman some illustrations and rhymes he had written.

> I had a beard and unwashed hair but Susan was incredibly gracious. She sat me down and began to read, and then she said: "Well, you're very talented and we'd like to publish you." I was stunned. "You mean you like my drawings?" I asked her, and she said, "Oh, no! You're the worst artist I've ever seen. But you have a natural gift here.
>
> To this day, I don't understand what she saw in those rhymes. But she sees things in people other editors miss. (cited in Horning 2001, 1)

Prelutsky has become a prolific children's poet; his playful and descriptive poems are a staple in many elementary classrooms and children's libraries. What did Hirschman see in Prelutsky's writing that Nordstrom didn't? Perhaps it would have been helpful to the publishing industry if Hirschman taught others to see what she saw—perhaps developing a catchy and marketable acronym to capture her insights. But then again, Richard Jackson—a well-respected editor at Simon and Schuster—attributes Hirschman's eye to something that can only belong to Hirshman: her own mind. Jackson says of Hirschman,

> She knows her own mind, which is awfully good and awfully helpful to someone who is young. When I first started working with her, I once brought her a manuscript by a well-known author. She took it home and read it, and brought it back and said: "But does it convince you?" and I thought, "Oh, boy, that is the question," but I hadn't thought to ask it. She planted in my mind a single question that has been there ever since and which is really important to the way I look at books. (cited in Horning 2001, 2)

From Hirschman, Jackson learned to pay attention to his own reaction to a piece of writing. Hirschman's question—"But does it convince you?"—implicates the reader in the assessment process. She didn't ask if the writing was organized, had voice, or excellent idea development. She asked if the piece of writing *convinced* him. To assess a piece of writing well, Hirschman seemed to be saying, Jackson needed to pay attention to how the piece of writing affected him.

To those of us schooled in the notion that fairness in education means standards that are external, clear, and committed to paper for all to see, strive for, and be judged by, Hirschman's reliance on her own mind and reactions seems arbitrary and full of unknowns. After all, how can an author know just what will convince Hirschman, or anyone else, for that matter? Since Hirschman's method doesn't honor the tenets of positivism, we dismiss it by saying that Hirschman is a master editor, an artist, a *magician* really. Let Hirschman wave her magic wand while the rest of us operate within clearer parameters.

But Hirschman is not the only proponent of readers who pay attention to an internal reaction not subject to the Holy Grail of Ideas, Organization, Form, Flavor, Mechanics, and Wording. In an email interview, Leigh Peake, the editorial director at Heinemann, often finds that she is more interested in a reviewer's "gut" than in the hours he or she might have spent carefully crafting answers to the list of questions that Heinemann sends to reviewers. She notes that

> [m]ore than once, a reviewer has written a carefully positive review, answering all of our questions, and then I'll get just a quick, one-line email saying something like, "You know, I just sent you my review, but I have to say that I didn't like the proposal very much." Often, I'll pay more attention to those gut responses than to the reviews they've written. Maybe the questions we asked didn't elicit what they thought. (2005)

Before we continue to look at how the publishing industry honors readers' minds, guts, and conflicting views when assessing working writers, it is worth remembering that we cannot simply translate everything that happens in the publishing industry into our classrooms. Just because publishers might send a curt rejection letter does not mean that we need to start creating curt rejection letters to students we have deemed writing failures. We are looking to the publishing industry to begin our search for more promising practices; we must still evaluate the assumptions behind publishing industry practices to make sure they mesh with our deepest convictions about the complexities of the writing process and our understandings of literacy pedagogy. Many editorial decisions are driven by market concerns. While we could loosely interpret "market" to mean "audience," this would be a dangerous oversimplification. More often than not, "market" means "bottom-line," and in this case, education has no business dabbling in the market. Our assessment decisions must be based on sound pedagogy, not on what is most likely to be purchased quickly because it is inexpensive or easy.

So how does Hirschman's focus on her own mind and Peake's attention to a reader's gut fit with what we know about the complexities of writing? Hirschman and Peake's attention to reader reactions—unmediated by rubrics—point to writing's rhetorical effect and purpose. When I write, I'm writing for a human being. I want to affect you or to figure out what I really think. When I write something, I think of the mind as a harp I've got to learn how to play. If my writing is good, I'll have masterfully plucked the strings of your brain—you'll have seen, heard, smelled, tasted, touched, and thought the same things that I have, and you'll have mixed it around with your knowledge and experiences to make something new. When I write well, you can hear this music—which is slightly different now than the music I set out to play, because now you're playing, too.

Throw a rubric on the table, and I'm writing for a piece of paper. This piece of paper has no life experience to mix up with mine, only out-of-tune strings named Tone, Style, and Organization, overused and on the verge of snapping if I pluck them too hard. I stop listening for the music when I write to the rubric, because paper doesn't vibrate or listen. When you use a rubric to tell me about my writing, you take your eyes off me and look at the rubric, modulating your tone to match the unresponsive categories.

When Hirschman listens to her mind and Peake listens to readers' gut responses, they are honoring the rhetorical purpose of writing. Opening the door to rhetorical purpose in writing assessment also opens the door to subjectivity, bringing us back to the dilemma that confronted Diederich and his ETS team in the 1950s: what do we do when readers disagree on a single piece of writing? If we honor positivism, we solve this problem by forcing agreement through the use of rubrics. If we honor the rhetorical purpose of writing, we solve this problem by helping students to wade through conflicting views of their work, honoring disagreement without getting lost in it.

How do we honor disagreement when assessing our own work—going so far as to elicit disagreement—without being paralyzed by it? When I asked for feedback on my introduction and first chapter of this book early in the writing process, I received several rounds of conflicting advice. Before sending out the proposal to Heinemann for review, I asked my life partner, a psychologist, and my friend, a writing teacher, to read the first two pages I had written about my writing retreat. My partner wasn't sure why I would begin a book about rubrics with a story about my writing weekend. He thought my first word should be *rubrics*. My friend, a writing teacher, disagreed. She said she was pulled in by the shared experience of a writing retreat, and she began to trust a voice that admitted its own failings. Given the conflicting readings, was one reader "wrong," and if so, how would I decide? I considered both readers intelligent, and I trusted that they both took their readings seriously—they were my "esteemed readers." In the end, I made my decision based on whose reading most closely resembled my intended audience; while my life partner is surely right about most everything else, I took my writing teacher friend's advice. I sent the proposal to Heinemann with the writing retreat intact.

Once Heinemann received my proposal, a similar conflict played itself out in the reviews. At Heinemann, when an editor receives a book proposal and decides it might be worth pursuing, she sends the proposal out to two outside reviewers, generally to a classroom teacher and to an expert in the area addressed by the proposal. My proposal was sent to Lind Williams, high school English teacher, and to Bob Broad, professor of English at Illinois State University and author of *What We Really Value: Beyond Rubrics in Teaching and Assessing Writing*. In his reader report for Heinemann, Broad wrote of my introduction,

> I applaud the author's critique of the bullying dynamic evident in our use of the phrase "best practice." Yet at the same time it felt to me that this section delayed the author from getting sooner in her introduction to the issue on which the book is focused: rubrics. . . . The "best practice" piece is an important section—the author provides a powerful and important vision of how teachers should engage what are presented to them as best practices. But I'm not sure it belongs in the early pages of the book's introduction, prior to any mention of rubrics.

Broad's review sent me into an obsessive spin. At the time he was the only author I'd found writing and thinking critically about rubrics. I'd spent months reading and rereading his work and envying his clarity. I was briefly tempted to do whatever he suggested. After all, he was an expert, right? Then I thought about Lind Williams' reaction to the same section in his reader report.

> This was a fascinating explication and helps to set up the critical inquiry into the use of rubrics. How do we know that any particular practice is the "best" practice? After the first chapter, I'm primed and ready for more investigation into theory until I eventually get to what she prefers to call "promising practices...."

When Lind wrote "I'm primed and ready for more investigation into theory," he did something incredibly helpful—he let me know how my writing *affected* him. From outside of the reading and writing experience, Broad's suggestion made perfect sense: why write about something without writing about it? But Lind let me know that as a reader, he needed to deconstruct the authority of best practice before he was ready to look more critically at rubrics. Broad, on the other hand, had spent his career thinking about these issues. He didn't need to be prepared for a critique of rubrics, so my introduction really did slow down his reading. But I wasn't writing primarily for writing assessment specialists. I was writing for teachers who might have doubts and confusion about writing assessment. I emailed my editor about Broad's suggestion,

> On one hand, he's completely right. How can you write the first eight pages of a book in which you completely ignore the subject of the book? On the other hand, IF I'm right to put it there (and this is a big IF, I realize) we can chalk up the disagreement to my better understanding of audience. Rubrics are so ingrained, that... I feel I have to "back into" a critique—and, as Lind says, "prime" the audience and leave the door open before I even mention rubrics.

Gloria responded,

> I was already arguing (internally) with Broad's judgment about the "best practices" stuff. Your analysis is perfect: the audience does require some foreplay. I'm sure you know this, but there's no One Best Way, ordained by the gods of objectivity, to write this book. Reviewers (and editors) bring their perspective, and we value them and give them serious consideration, but your own judgment is the one to be honored.

In the end, I found comfort in Gloria's agreement with me. But this agreement had come after serious critical thinking about my audience and purposes—prompted by disagreement—thinking that clarified my entire approach to the book. In other words, I needed both positions fully articulated before I could come to a decision that worked for me.

By placing the onus on the writer to sift through conflicting judgments, we are asking writers to peel back the layers that create our assessments. Although our acceptance of disagreement has opened the door to subjectivity, our shift from agreement at all costs allows us to deal head-on with the nature of how readers interact with writing—its rhetorical effect and purpose. In this way, our assessments and instruction acknowledge the complexity of the writing process. In this acknowledgment, we make our assessment process transparent, talking and thinking through what goes on in our minds as we follow our students' words—a process we used to mask by focusing on how our students met the external standards of the rubric. Without the forced agreement of the rubric, we keep our minds open to new insights about writing, and encourage our students to do the same. In essence, we are acknowledging assessment as an integral part of the writing process rather than what we do after the writing process is "complete."

In an assessment process unconstrained by premature agreement, our unobstructed view of how writing and reading really work supports students and teachers. Louann Reid, editor of NCTE's *English Journal*, describes the importance of an assessment process that honors dissent.

> Sending the articles out for review is not only an important part of the process, but it's an essential feature of my editing philosophy. First, I envision *English Journal* as a forum for conversations among educators. So it's necessary to have readers who are in classrooms other than mine reading manuscripts and offering feedback from their perspective. Second, reviewing provides excellent professional development for both the reviewer and the writer. Reviewers tell me that they enjoy seeing all the new ideas and that they get a sense of satisfaction in suggesting changes that will make a manuscript better, even if it will be sent to another journal when *EJ* can't use it. We annually send reviewers who want it a collection of all of the reviews on the manuscripts they reviewed so they can see how their reviews compare to those from other readers.

We almost always receive conflicting reviews, but if the conflicts are not extreme, I pay more attention to the comments that the reviewer sends and to what I know about the reviewer. Reviewers can recommend three actions—reject, accept with revisions, accept. We occasionally receive all three recommendations when we send to three reviewers. Some authors of articles we cannot use write to express their gratitude—and surprise—for the extensive comments they receive. I use the reviewers' comments to help me select articles and then to suggest revisions to the authors. So they are absolutely useful to me.

Writers tell me that they are grateful for the feedback on their articles even when we cannot use them. This review process engages a professional community in conversation and educates and affirms writers. (2005)

Imagine that: a writing assessment process that "engages a professional community in conversation and educates and affirms writers." If writing assessment is to accomplish all of this—and honor the Golden Rule of Writing Assessment—we will need principles other than reliability to guide us. In an attempt to more closely match writing assessment with our pedagogical values based in constructivism and a contextual paradigm, I propose the following list of principles:

Writing Assessment Principles Grounded in Contextual and Constructivist Paradigms

♦ Honor **rhetorical purpose and effect**—the way that words affect a reader's mind—and encourage writers to understand that writing is assessed by readers who bring different understandings and experiences to their readings and assessment.

♦ Assessment should be **responsive** and **encourage new insights**— it should allow us to identify our values in reaction to a specific piece of writing. Therefore, we must teach readers (including ourselves!) to pay attention to what they think and feel as they read and to explain their reactions in helpful ways to authors—a **metacognitive reading**.

♦ Understand disagreement by exploring a reader's context and the author's purpose. If we encourage readers to pay attention to their reactions to writing, we open the door to **disagreement**. Dealing with disagreements means exploring a reader's **position or context**: what experiences, background, or assumptions lead a reader to a particular assessment?

♦ **Encourage readers to articulate their positions.** In this way, we shift the responsibility of transparency from the clear external standards of rubrics to the internal standards, assumptions, and experience that readers bring to their readings and assessments.

♦ Teach student authors **how to extract clarity from disagreement** through careful study of readers' context and their own purposes. After studying dissent and where it comes from, the author is in a better position to understand and articulate how these views fit or do not fit into the author's intent.

In teaching—a lonely profession—rubric norming sessions brought writing teachers together to have valuable discussions about writing, but let us not accept an assessment tool that cuts our discussions short for the sake of agreement. Let's take our conversations further, honor the rhetorical purpose of writing, and agree to disagree for the sake of insight.

Making Our Subjectivity Transparent and Useful

What Response Unmediated by Rubrics Looks Like in Our Classrooms

What really helps me to write is when people give
really specific things that sound good or not—
because I can't tell. I know what I mean; I just need
to know if other people know what I mean. A rubric
doesn't help me know any of that.

—SASHA ACKER, AGE SEVENTEEN

John regularly wreaked havoc in my classroom, spinning wildly on my stool, scratching random vulgarities into desks, tipping over chairs, and whipping up his dirty T-shirt to show anyone willing to look how he'd carved the word *hate* into his side with a homemade tattoo device involving a nail and a hairdryer motor. As the year progressed, even the most heart-wrenching stories I heard about John's life outside of school couldn't mitigate the dread I felt when he walked into my classroom. Apparently, the other students felt the same way. John would attach himself to people, follow them around asking inane questions, sit and stand too close for comfort, poke them with paperclips or his pencil, and sometimes explode unpredictably and threaten to kill himself and others. On at least three occasions, John was beat up behind the school building during breaks. He came back to class, bloody and sniffling, refusing to talk or to clean up.

Nothing worked: admonitions, redirections, pats on the back, calls home, referrals to counselors, detentions, suspensions, meetings with the district social worker. No one could figure out what to do with John, but everyone was working on it, so there was little to do but

66

endure. After he had nagged Mandy, a particularly patient student nearly to the point of blows, I approached John.

"Why do you do that?" I asked.

"Do what?" John asked with wide eyes.

"You know, bug people." As if he didn't know.

"I wasn't bugging nobody. I was just trying to be friendly."

Trying to be *friendly?* I'd been assuming that John knew exactly what he was doing, that he was trying to make us crazy. But if John were telling the truth—and his face and voice seemed painfully sincere—I'd have to see John for what he was: a sad, lonely kid with no understanding of how he affected other people.

For people like John, social interaction can be painfully confusing. Our reactions to others are complex, nuanced, changeable depending on context—they are, in fact, subjective. To compound the problem, these reactions remain largely unarticulated. Most of us are savvy enough to understand anyway, but those who don't receive little helpful feedback. The rules of politeness keep us from saying exactly what we think, so those who most need meaningful feedback about their behavior get the least: some distance themselves through cruelty or rejection, while some, like Mandy, try to be nice, reinforcing annoying behavior by suffering in silence. I'd been trying to address John's behavior through external rules: *Don't poke people.* But if I wanted to help John interact in ways that allowed him to make the friends he wanted, maybe I'd have to address John's behavior from the inside, beginning with a clear, kind, honest articulation of how his actions impacted others.

"John, I think you're a good person, and I really want you to get along with other people. And I think other people want to like you too, but sometimes you do things that make it difficult—things that really annoy people. So can I tell you what Mandy might have been thinking when you were talking to her asking her questions just a moment ago?"

John looked at me oddly but nodded.

"I was watching. Mandy had her head down, writing. You walked up, put your head halfway into her desk, and said 'Hi!'"

"Yup, told you I was trying to be friendly!"

"I know. And that was a friendly thing to say. And Mandy thought so too—she looked up and said hello back. But then she put her head back down and started writing while you kept talking and asking her questions. What do you think she was trying to tell you?"

John said he didn't know, so I described the entire interaction I'd witnessed, trying to put into words what might have been going through Mandy's mind. John listened, puzzled. When our conversation was over, he thanked me and went on his way.

I continued to watch John. I'd like to say he was voted Most Popular as a result of my little intervention. Of course he wasn't, and I frequently had to pull him aside and talk him through how his actions were actually keeping him from making the friends he so badly needed. But he was trying, and I watched his growing awareness of what others wanted, cutting his inappropriate ramblings short by muttering "I guess I'll let you work now." Better yet, I saw him engaged in more conversations with people who were interested in what he was saying. On the last day of school, I complimented him for being able to hear some difficult feedback from me and being willing to try so hard. He smiled. "Thank *you*. What you said really helped me."

Our ability to teach students to write more effectively depends equally on two factors: our students' desire to be understood, and clear, kind, honest articulation of how their words affect us. Like the rules of social interaction, the factors that influence our evaluations and assessments of what we read are complex, nuanced, and changeable depending on context. In other words, they are subjective. Because our educational testing theory is based on reliability and objectivity, we have tried to solidify and externalize our reactions to students' writing by using a rubric—which is ultimately impossible, since our reactions happen privately in the subjective silence and context of our minds.

In fact, if you've ever tried to incorporate peer revision into your writing classes, you've probably battled students' tendency toward vague, subjective assessments—"I liked it, I guess." You might have imposed bans on such statements of liking or given up peer revision altogether because it is so difficult: students don't know how to assess or respond to each other's work very well. They've heard the rules for good writing: organization, word choice, sentence fluency. But like John, hearing or knowing these rules doesn't prepare them to respond to the complex nuances and contexts provided by each new piece of writing. They're used to approaching writing from the outside: *The writing is organized or it isn't*. But these responses and assessments don't help students develop real insights about writing or revise their writing in ways that honor rhetorical purpose and effect. They aren't used to approaching writing from the inside—being asked to articulate

what goes on in their minds when they read each other's work. Brian
Huot suggests that,

> [C]urrent classroom practices require evaluative skills from students
> which we do not, for the most part, teach . . . most student revision
> centers on correctness, since the value of correct writing has been
> emphasized over and over again in various assessment, testing and
> grading contexts. We need to recognize that before students can learn
> to revise rhetorically, they must assess rhetorically. Certainly, much
> current writing instruction focuses on rhetorical concepts, but there is
> no clear evidence that our assessment of student writing focuses on
> these same criteria. In fact, large scale research into teacher response
> (Connors and Lunsford 1993) as well as classroom-based research
> (Sperling 1994) seems to indicate that teachers do not respond to and
> evaluate student writing rhetorically. (2002a, 68–69)

Perhaps we haven't taught students to respond rhetorically because
our assessment tools don't prepare us to develop and model these
responses.

I wanted my assessments and assignments to honor the rhetorical
purpose of writing, be meaningful, to match writing pedagogy, and to
avoid reductionism. I was ready to let rubrics go and see what would
happen in Krystal and Felicity's Personal Narratives class without them.
I was afraid that I might be left with a vague feeling: *Your writing makes
me really sad* or *I can't stop thinking about how you laugh and make faces
while I talk, so your writing makes me angry.* But the case against rubrics
was too overwhelming to avoid the risk, and this class was the perfect
place to begin pursuing more promising practices: the students were
finding their writing so meaningful that we had decided to turn them
into a public performance at the end of the year. But what would it look
like if I took my own advice and assessed writing in a way that honored
the rhetorical purpose of writing?

It was less than six weeks before our performance, and my students
were glaring at me. In fact, they were staging a sort of coup. We had
spent the entire semester writing about our lives and crafting these writings into a script that to date included Krystal's writing about thunderstorms, a bit of guerilla theater put together by three teen mothers in
the class, Maria's exploration of body image, modern dance performed
to Denni's poetry, and Travers' reflections of how his father's death
made him evaluate his own life. These disparate writings had come

together in our minds when Denni had shared something she had written about her difficulty expressing her thoughts out loud: "So my mind forced a new way of voice and thought. I find it hard to resist a pen. Emotions bursts from it so easily, and all I have to do is follow the mind. It is how you are seeing a piece of my soul without even knowing who I am. Each letter holds out its meanings to the world, and if people don't think it's important enough, I write it louder." Based on Denni's idea that art can make public our most private thoughts, we'd named the performance "Louder!," and our script was becoming a collage of the stories that lurk beneath the surface of our lives.

The beginning of our script needed a new transition, so I had written a short piece to fill the gap. I read the piece to the students, they made a few revisions, and Faith was recording it for a voice-over. She had already practiced reading it several times for the class when I asked her to stop for a moment and read more slowly. She tried again, and I stopped her once more. "Even more slowly," I urged. She looked confused, and the class was storming to her defense. One student rolled her eyes and said that it sounded fine. Why should Faith do it again?

I knew the piece didn't sound right to me yet, but I wasn't sure I could explain why. I needed to figure it out quickly—one frustrated student was getting up to leave the room. Why did I hear what was wrong while they didn't? I knew that none of my students had performance experience, and most hadn't ever been to the theater save the school auditorium for the sixth-grade play. They didn't yet think like an audience.

"Trust me for a minute and close your eyes," I pleaded. The student at the door narrowed her eyes at me but nonetheless plopped down defiantly at a desk. "You've heard this piece at least ten times today, and you're sick of it, aren't you?" They nodded and harumphed. "Since you've heard it so many times, you want Faith to read it as quickly as possible to get it over with. But I want you to try to imagine that you're sitting in the audience on the night of the performance. The stage is dark, and Faith's voice is the only thing you hear. You've *never* heard these words before. I'm going to read this piece two different ways, and I want you to pay close attention to what you're thinking as I read."

I read the piece slowly, pausing after particularly rich phrases, savoring the best words and ideas. I looked around. Thankfully, students' eyes were closed. They were either sleeping or listening carefully. I started to read the piece again—with plenty of expression, but without any of the pauses. I looked around again, and several brows were furrowed—a good sign. When I finished, students opened their eyes and looked at me expectantly. Crisis averted.

"What did you notice?"

Silence.

"Which reading was better?"

"The slower one. It was way better," Faith said. The class was nodding in agreement.

"Why?"

Silence.

From their faces, I knew they felt the difference, even if they couldn't put it into words yet. I could relate; several moments before I hadn't been able to either. I ventured my own reaction.

"When Faith read the first line, it was so full of images that I needed a moment to think about it. When she read it fast, I was still thinking about the last line she read and I missed all the other lines. In fact, I got a little angry. I needed time to catch up with the words, and I found myself begging her not to say anything more. When I'm reading, I can go at my own pace, but when I'm listening, I'm completely at the mercy of the speaker. Are they going to give me the time I need, or not? If not, I'm lost."

Class had ended during my explanation, and as students left the room, they were all speaking at once. "That's it!" "Yeah, I couldn't hear the ending because . . . " "I just wanted a minute!"

When they came back the next day to record, Faith nailed her reading, prompting exclamations of awe and congratulations from the class. As we began to read and talk through the script again, they began spontaneously talking through their reactions to it. Not only were they giving each other meaningful feedback, they were taking over the class, and this time, I didn't mind at all. I removed myself from our customary circle of chairs and sat behind my desk for the first time all semester, smiling as I listened to Maria tell Travers that she felt edgy when he paced back and forth while he read his lines: Did he intend for us to think he was nervous? Perhaps he should think about when he wanted us to feel nervous, and pace only then.

The strategy of articulating what goes on in our minds when we read and write has been used by English teachers for years. Teachers regularly model their own responses to literature, using think-alouds to show students how we layer our experiences, knowledge, questions, and frustrations onto the words we read. Think-alouds fit beautifully into the constructivist paradigm, illustrating reader response theory by showing students how we construct meaning from literature and our lives. In addition, many teachers use think-alouds to reveal what goes on in their minds while they write—talking through the choices they make during the composing process. Writing teachers also routinely ask students to write about their own process of writing and include these reflective pieces in portfolios or writer's notebooks. After witnessing firsthand the impact of talking through my reactions to Faith's performance pace, I was anxious to apply this strategy to writing assessment. Would articulating my response to writing help students revise just as effectively?

Maria provided me with a perfect opportunity to apply a metacognitive response to writing. She came to my room during lunch to talk about a piece she was working on titled "Uniquely Me." Maria read out loud,

> Through your eyes, I see my wide hips. You see my obscene arms with my dark hair and my dark eyebrows. But I think of my *abuela* who gives me the power of never-ending acceptance, love, and pride. Through my reflection I see my dark roots, I see my light split-ends in which I dyed. I see that my dark hair is coming back darker than before. It refuses to hide and I don't want it to anymore. Through my footsteps I feel my extra weight, but in return it gives me warmth, and that is something I won't trade for the imagination picture of a portrait. When I take my picture, I want it to be me. I don't want it to be the products you see on T.V., because I am uniquely Cuban, uniquely me.

As I listened to Maria read, I was delighted to hear her make the connection between her acceptance of herself and her grandmother's acceptance of her. But I realized that as I was listening to her words, I was layering the richness of another piece she had written earlier in the year about the first day she met her grandmother and how she and her grandmother talk on the phone every week even though they don't speak the same language; my initial response was taking into account words and images that weren't there yet.

After I expressed my delight in where Maria was headed in her writing, I decided to withhold my insight to see what would happen if I gave Maria space to come to her own reaction. I asked her what images and memories she was seeing as she read the words she'd actually written. Maria thought for a moment, then smiled and rummaged through her notebook. "I gotta give the audience what I know, right?" she asked as she handed me the earlier piece she'd written about her grandmother.

When Maria and I talked through the images and memories that she wanted her writing to elicit, she was able to see what was missing from the words she'd actually put on the page—an understanding that Maria would not have developed from a rubric category such as "Attention to detail" or "Rich images." When we help students to think through the associations that they and their readers make, we are not only honoring the rhetorical purpose of writing but we are also acknowledging the complex nature of language itself. I remember being intrigued in my first linguistics course when my professor drew on the board two conflicting models of how we process language. The first model looked very much like a dictionary: on one side of the board was the word *grandmother*, and across from it was the phrase, *one of our parents' mothers*. According to this model of language processing, we hear a word and we access the definition, fitting this definition into the structure of whatever sentence it is in. This model didn't feel right to me; it didn't seem to reflect how my mind worked.

The second model looked more complex and felt closer to my experience of language. The professor drew a conglomeration of overlapping circles—each with a word or phrase in the middle. In the center circle he wrote the word *grandmother*. For every person, the surrounding web of circles would be slightly different: my own would include words and images such as *gingersnaps* and *knitting* and *talcum powder* and *gold-speckled mint green countertops* and *lilacs* and *rusty swing set*. Linked to the "knitting" circle might be a cluster of circles with words and images such as *purple scarf* and *wrinkled hands*. Overlapping the "wrinkled hand" circle might be the words *blue veins* and *cancer* and *fear of death*. The second model captured the associative nature of language—the evocative power of words. It explained why I smell gingersnaps and hear a rusty swing set and feel a pang of loss when I read the word *grandmother*. And this model helped me to explain to Maria what words, phrases, and stories her reader needed to see in order to understand the connection between her grandmother and her self-image as she did.

With a deeper understanding of what she wanted her words to evoke, Maria worked for a week on revisions. The first revision she handed me after combing the two pieces of writing was clunky; she'd taken huge risks, stretching way beyond her comfort zone. While her revision was less clear and powerful than either her initial writing about her grandmother or her first draft of "Uniquely Me," the potential in the new revision was exciting. I asked her to read it out loud again and to think through where the audience might zone out because they'd already "gotten" an idea or image from something else she'd written, suggesting that she consider which description was the most powerful and cutting the description that wasn't necessary. Finally, she brought in this version.

> Through your eyes, I see my wide hips. You see my obscene arms with my dark hair and dark eyebrows. But I think of my grandmother—my *abuela*—and the first day I met her. I remember how she came and hugged me tightly. I could see the love in her eyes. I had never met her, but somehow, I knew that this woman was something special to me. I could see that she had been waiting a long time for me.
>
> My grandmother's hair was sprayed in place—immovable. She sat me on her lap in the living room chair close enough so I could feel her breath crash against my body. My grandmother gently brushed my hair. With each brush stroke she took, my head gently slid back. She sat there for at least forty minutes brushing and drying my hair, and it felt like an eternity of belonging.
>
> My grandmother and I do not speak the same language. Even so, she still tells me she loves me in Spanish—*yo taykeatomucho Maria*—and the most magnificent smile comes over her face every time she sees me. I wonder what we would talk about if she could speak English. I wonder what it was like coming to America from Cuba. I wonder if she remembers the day she brushed my hair as vividly as I do.
>
> My *abuela* gives me my pride and strength. Through my grandmother's eyes, I see my dark hair coming back darker than before. It refuses to hide. Through my footsteps I feel my extra weight, but in return it gives me warmth, and that is something I will not trade. When you take my picture, I want it to be me. Because I am uniquely Cuban, uniquely me.

When Maria read me this version, we looked at each other with a mutual recognition that she had done it—to use Denni's words, she had shown her readers a piece of her soul. I didn't need to write a single word of feedback on this final draft; she and I both knew how powerful it was.

I asked Maria to share all of her versions with the class and talk through how she made decisions about what to change or cut. I was worried at first; this class had a notoriously short attention span, and I hoped they would give Maria their respectful attention. I shouldn't have worried. They responded to Maria's words and the struggle she'd gone through to get them right, listening carefully. Afterward, they dug into their own revisions with purpose and attention that I hadn't seen in them before. They truly wanted their audience to understand, and once they started thinking about how the audience might be reacting to their words, they filled in gaps, cut out needless repetition, and combined writing pieces they'd worked on throughout the semester. In fact, one student who had refused to write at all brought in a wonderful piece of writing about her own body image, and tried not to act thrilled when the class clamored to add it to the script.

We never used the terms *organization*, *word choice*, or *voice*. The only common language about writing we developed in class revolved around the idea of making our private responses to words public—making our subjectivity transparent and useful. Though students rearranged their writing, thought carefully about what words would express what they thought, and emerged as real people through their writing, they accomplished this by thinking through and comparing what they wanted to express with how their words would filter through someone else's mind. In this way, they directly accessed the rhetorical heart of writing. Since we bypassed the outward markers of good writing—the reductive categories on which rubrics are based—our insights and assessments about writing came straight from the complex nature of writing, reading, and response. After their performance, which brought everyone in the audience to tears, Maria wrote,

> Before we knew it, a lot of students in the class were getting deeper and more expressive in their writing. We all realized that we had something to say, and that's what led to the idea of how we were going to say it to other people. The preparation of a performance began—our message, to last forever . . . .
>
> I learned things in this class that I never really knew before and things that will help me and stay with me until my death. I found how to express myself better and to have pride in myself. That is something I never could do before. I saw the inside story of real life. I hope that our message was sent on to our audience, to everyone who ever hears about the performance of little-town Journey High School's Personal Narratives Class.

It was no accident that I was able to help students think through an audience's response to their performance before I was able to use this kind of metacognitive response to help Maria assess and revise her writing. The audience for the performance was authentic and tangible.

Too often in schools, the artificiality of our writing assignments masks writing's rhetorical purpose. Consider the predicament of the student who is told to write to a state-standardized writing assessment prompt—"Your school is in a funding crisis. They must cut programs. Write to the local school board, convincing them that they should either cut art or physical education classes." At first this seems like an "authentic" writing prompt—a real-life problem that solicits a real-life answer. It could be worse—"Write about *Justice*." But its artificiality is revealed when the student raises his hand and asks in excitement, "Is the school board going to read this?" When you tell him that no, in fact his essay will be outsourced to a paid reader, perhaps someone in Indiana or Ohio whom he will never meet, and who has no intention of making a decision about the fate of his beloved art classes, his face drops and he halfheartedly writes his answer.

The student understands, without knowing the jargon, that the rhetorical context of the writing prompt has been lost. The paid reader in Indiana is reading for whatever categories are on the state assessment program rubric: style, voice, organization, mechanics. The reader does not ultimately care what the student has to say, nor, for that matter, does the student. The student's intention and the reader's reaction are practically nonexistent, and any assessment that follows is meaningless. Were the local school board really in a budget crisis, anxious to read his proposal, ask him questions, and form a decision, not only would the student's writing rise to the occasion, but his expectation of assessment and feedback would change.

Consider the logical progression of this lack of concern for the rhetorical purpose of writing that schools have accepted and perpetuated: it began with Diederich and his colleagues' distrust of the responses of their fifty-three esteemed readers and the team's attempt to reduce, align, and externalize their insights about writing into a standardized list of five "factors of writing." Later, the organization of these factors into the performance levels on a matrix cemented this distrust of writing's rhetorical effect by forcing teachers to disregard their responses to writing in deference to the rubric. The logical conclusion of this fear of our own reactions is the computer grading program, poised to completely and forever strip the humanity from writing and response. Criterion, ETS's entry into the computer grading market, promises teachers and students almost instantaneous feedback and evaluation based on a four- or six-point rubric, rubrics based on Diederich and the team's work over a half century ago. The computer program claims validity because trained readers agree with its evaluation "almost all the time." But as we've already seen, the trained readers agree because they're given a narrow definition of good writing and formula for grading it. Either the computer grading system is as "good" as human readers, or the human readers are trained to read like an unresponsive computer. At the heart of this training is the rubric.

Most criticism of computer grading systems has focused on how easy it is to trick them into giving a nonsensical paper that uses big words and sophisticated construction a high score. But even if computer grading programs become savvy enough to see through these attempts, the entire premise that a computer could assess writing undermines writing's rhetorical purpose. How ridiculous would it be to look deep into your computer screen, profess love for it, and have your computer assess your sincerity? Even with minute calculations of facial expression and intonation, the entire scenario is based on an absurd premise, rendering the action and assessment ludicrous. Using computers to grade our students' writing is no different—the computer does not care what the students have to say or how they say it, so why should the students care?

As if in anticipation of this criticism, the FAQ section of Criterion's website asks, "How do students feel about being graded by a computer program?" Their answer attempts to placate without addressing the criticism underlying the question: "Most of today's students have had experience with instant feedback in computer programs and are very comfortable with the idea of computerized scoring." But writing is not a game, and being eaten in a game of Pac-Man is far different feedback than the kind required when we ask students to communicate their thoughts and observations to an audience. Ignoring the rhetorical purpose of writing cheapens and dehumanizes what should be an important and humanizing task.

When teachers consistently assign writing they have no interest in reading and assume the role of readers they are not, students understand the dishonesty of the exercise and the feedback. Worse yet, they may begin pandering to the teacher's taste, thereby undermining the awareness of diverse audiences they must gain in authentic writing situations. Without a real audience, or investment enough in the topic that the imagined audience feels real, why not write for external standards such as "organization" or "style"?

Since we cannot separate our assessments from the entire context of our writing instruction, it does little good to articulate our reactions to writing in which students have no investment. Just as a whole-language approach to teaching—grounded in constructivism and a contextual paradigm—recognizes that phonics instruction is not powerful unless students are immersed in meaningful literacy experiences, an assessment process that compares a student's purpose in writing with its effect on a reader's mind is not powerful unless students have meaningful contexts for writing and exploring their purposes in writing. Unless we plan to address our students' investment in their writing and our investment in reading student work on the state, district, and classroom level, rethinking rubrics is pointless. But without addressing these issues, our students' writing and our reading and assessment of that writing are meaningless. And what is the point of writing and reading other than to construct and access meaning?

But How Shall We Grade?

Investing in Process for the Sake of Product

The relation of thought to word is not a thing but a process, a continual movement back and forth from thought to word and from word to thought. In that process the relation of thought to word undergoes changes. . . . Thought is not merely expressed in words; it comes into existence through them. Every thought tends to connect something with something else, to establish a relationship between things. Every thought moves, grows and develops . . .

—Lev Vygotsky (1962)

My goal in eleventh grade was to become a fast swimmer. I'd always enjoyed swimming, and I'd raced my friend Sarah every day during our summers spent at the local public pool. I fancied myself fast because my need to win far surpassed hers, churning my arms through the water in fantastic desperate pinwheels that generally kept me a stroke or two ahead.

When I took a Red Cross Lifeguard Certification course in high school, I encountered truly fast swimmers: girls who had spent large portions of their lives in Speedos competing on private swim teams. I was stunned by how smoothly they swam. I had always equated speed with visible effort; my cheerful pummeling should by all rights secure me many victories. But I thrashed through lap after lap day after day next to these smooth-muscled swimming machines only to emerge panting—from water which was clearly not my friend—at least half an hour after they had finished their assigned mile. I was frustrated, but mostly confused: what did they know that I didn't?

After barely securing my life-guarding certificate I enrolled in the Water Instructor Safety course and began to learn how to teach various strokes. I discovered that there were actually techniques—S-shaped pulls designed to maximize the properties of water and resistance. I began experimenting at the local pool after school. I was furious at first, because when I concentrated on my pull, I lost what little speed I had. Several times I gave up, reverting once again to my old bumbling pace. But I swallowed my pride, deciding to slow down for the sake of technique. It took a whole summer, and I never did manage to join the ranks of girls who glided, but I gained speed and efficiency. More importantly, by investing in the process of swimming instead of the product of speed, I learned how the water works and how I could work with it.

I experience a similar pull between product and process when I write. I wrote the first four chapters of this book in the middle of the school year, leaving myself five chapters to write in the two summer months before my deadline. I made the mistake of doing the math: if I left myself time for revisions, I would need to write a chapter a week. Impossible! I wanted to diffuse my anxiety by focusing on the product, writing only within the structure of a chapter, skipping my customary prechapter ramblings. These musings were often messy, unfocused, and didn't look much like the writing that goes into a chapter, so I was tempted to bypass them.

However, I trusted the writing process enough to step back from the chapter at hand and freewrite whatever I was thinking or wondering about writing and assessment. I might throw this writing out later, but I knew that without it, my writing is often dry and stilted. My investment in the process might slow me down but would eventually strengthen the product. Ironically, engaging in these freewrites often jumpstarted my progress in particularly difficult chapters, guiding me gently around the dread of writer's block.

As those who have ever cleaned the inside of their kitchen cupboards can attest, things often get messier before they get better. Unless we are willing to dump the three open bags of powdered sugar and ancient package of larvae-infested flour onto the counters—consolidating, throwing away, and rearranging as we go—only the surface of the kitchen appears clean. The writing process is similar: Maria's revision of "Uniquely Me" (Chapter 6) got worse before it got better. She and I needed to trust the time it took her to search every corner of her mind, haphazardly pulling out, combining, and throwing away stored images before her finished writing could reflect the richness of her experiences. We have to be willing to trust the process to improve the product.

Secondary writing teachers—particularly high school teachers—often teach students only for brief intervals. We don't have the luxury of seeing the big picture: how a student's investment in the process translates into the hills and valleys of their written products. We would all probably agree that ranking or grading a student's draft-in-progress every ten minutes is akin to walking into the kitchen in the middle of spring cleaning and proclaiming it a hopeless mess. For this reason, many of us only grade the final version of a paper, recognizing that grading every draft doesn't accurately represent our students' efforts or encourage revision. Some of us only grade end-of-course portfolios, giving students permission to allow their writing to get messier before it gets better and to choose the pieces of writing in which they've invested the most and which represent their best efforts.

But withholding a grade until the very end of the course sometimes violates school policy. Teachers at my district's junior high are required to hand out computer-generated grade strips to students every week, in a laudable (if sometimes misguided) effort to keep students informed and involved in their progress. If we don't grade every draft, or even every final draft, what do we grade?

Linda Christensen, author of *Writing, Reading and Rising Up*, founding editor of *Rethinking Schools*, and language arts coordinator for Portland Public Schools in Oregon, admits her dirty little secret: she hasn't graded a student paper in twenty-eight years. In "Moving Beyond Judgment," Christensen (2004–2005) explains her grading system,

> Because I work in public schools that still churn out report cards, I must give students grades at the end of each quarter and semester. And I do—based on the total points earned for each grading period. The difference is that I don't put grades on individual papers. (And I don't give quizzes or tests, nor do I assign or accept extra credit work.) They receive all of the credit possible or they redo the papers. For example, a first draft of an essay is typically 150 points; a revision is 300 points. But they only receive the points—all the points—if they write a paper that meets the criteria.

Christensen's Grading Policy

Grades: Your grades will be based on a number of criteria:

Basics Concepts of Class: In order to pass this class, you must demonstrate that you have learned the major concepts of the course. These will change from quarter to quarter, but sample outcomes might include writing an essay that demonstrates your understanding of historical or literary material or using historical facts to critique a document.

Completion of Daily Work: Daily work is the place we practice the skills needed for learning long-term skills. On a basketball court, team members might learn passing skills. In here, you will learn how to write at the college level by completing shorter writing assignments first or by completing a reading journal in preparation for writing an essay about a novel.

Class Participation: This class demands that you participate not only by completing the work, but also by contributing to class discussions. You contribute by listening while others speak, giving positive feedback, speaking on topic, learning how to take turns talking, taking notes during discussion that will help you write later, disagreeing with ideas rather than people. You also contribute by respecting other members of the class. No one should feel vulnerable in this room. We learn best in an atmosphere of tolerance where people can take risks. So expect positive, rather than negative, critique from your classmates and me.

Homework: Homework is an extension of the work in class. Often it will only be relevant in the context of our class work. For example, if we are studying welfare reform or the politics of language and you don't do the reading, you will not be able to participate or understand the class discussion related to the reading. Similarly, we will write essays, narratives, or poetry that parallel our reading assignments. If you do not do your homework, you will miss the connection.

Difficulty: There will be times when emergencies come up or when you do not understand the homework. In the event this happens, call me at home and I will either grant you more time or explain the work more thoroughly. You may also set up appointments to work with me after school or during lunch.

Extensions: Because I expect quality work, from time to time I will return your essays, narratives, and poetry so you can take more time to polish or rework them. I don't expect you all to be Alice Walkers, but I do expect that you will take time to learn how to write—which means learning how to rewrite. I will teach you, but in order to learn, you must practice. (33–37)

Christensen's grading system deftly negotiates our responsibility to "churn out report cards" and our responsibility to make our grades reflect what we value. The teacher is free to assess student writing without the continual burden of ranking—to articulate his or her responses to students' words, to examine the difference between what the student intended and what the writing actually accomplished. The student is free to take risks—to engage in the formative exchange between thought and language where we understand what we are saying only through the act of saying it—where our understandings shift as we experiment with ways to say what we think. In fact, the student is rewarded to take these risks, since this exploration is part of the writing process, and we have recognized its value by grading it.

This emphasis on process leaves teachers free to encourage, praise, and support risks that turn out badly, something I do intuitively with my eight-year-old son who is learning to skateboard. Last year, he worked hard on just being able to balance and turn. This year, he called me outside to watch him take a running start down the driveway, jump on his skateboard, and rapidly approach the curb on the other side of the street. As he tripped over the curb and sprawled across the sidewalk tangled up in his board, I grimaced. But I noticed that he was smiling. He hadn't randomly crashed; he was trying to "grind" the curb, jumping himself and the skateboard onto the edge of cement and sliding along it before jumping back either on the street or on the sidewalk. I stifled my concern long enough to celebrate his crash, vowing under my breath to buy him thicker kneepads. Did my son fail his trick? Yes. But was he doing exactly what he should be doing to learn to skateboard? Yes again. He didn't need his crash to be criticized; he needed his risk to be encouraged.

Now, if I knew more about skateboarding, I might talk with my son about what went wrong and what he might try differently next time. But I wouldn't describe his crash in detail and expect this to help: *your knee is bleeding and your skateboard is underneath your right arm which is twisted beneath your left leg.* I'd focus on describing what got him there: *your balance was good at first but you rushed your takeoff.* Because I do know about writing, I have a responsibility to talk with my students about what works in their writing and what they might try differently next time: *You started your research without thinking, talking, or writing about why bioethics matter to you. Doing that might help you make your paper more engaging.* Grading process instead of product isn't a way of smiling vaguely and indulgently and saying, "That's great, honey" in response to everything little Johnny does. Instead, it encourages students to try the things that will ultimately help them become better writers. When we grade every paper—or when we criticize every crash—we ignore and undermine what we know about the learning process in our insatiable need to rank every performance.

Despite its emphasis on process, Christensen's grading policy does give the teacher a limited role as gatekeeper: "Because I expect quality work, from time to time I will return your essays, narratives, and poetry so you can take more time to polish or rework them." In the act of returning the writing, the teacher has determined that the paper doesn't meet some minimum expectation of the class or that it doesn't represent the student's best efforts; students can't stare out of the window all hour, claim that they're brainstorming, hand in a one-paragraph paper, and expect an A+ because they "engaged in process." By passing or failing students, teachers act as gatekeepers between courses, shifting our responsibility to rank every paper to our ability to provide appropriate placement for students.

No matter how many revisions they go through and how much constructive feedback I give, I recognize that some of the students in my eleventh-grade writing class are not yet ready for the demands of my department's college-level, twelfth-grade research-based writing course. But determining what is an acceptable effort for an eleventh grader within my department is a far more reasonable task than distinguishing between the thirteen shades of achievement in a typical A to F scale—or worse yet, the one hundred possible shades of achievement implied by percentages. Truly, what is the difference between an 89 percent paper and a 90 percent paper? The distinction is ludicrous and dishonest.

Determining whether a student writer is ready for a certain writing course involves departmental conversations. For several years, I taught narrative and description-based writing courses with a brief foray into informational writing—a feeder course for the twelfth-grade research writing courses that my colleague Laura taught. As a new teacher, I worried that my focus on description and narrative might not adequately prepare students for Laura's class. Over the course of several conversations about our classes and expectations, she assured me that while she considered it her job to teach the technical aspects of research writing, she appreciated and valued the confident voices and investment in process that my students were bringing to her class.

Despite recognizing our limited role as gatekeepers between courses, Christensen's grading policy mostly focuses on students' engagement in the writing process and provides context for the one-dimensional act of ranking students' writing. We regularly take context into account when we make placement decisions—we say things such as, "Peter's writing isn't as good as Susan's, but he works incredibly hard and doesn't get frustrated easily—I think he's ready for your class with some extra help." In addition to honoring the efforts of struggling writers, our focus on process gives us room to respond effectively to truly gifted writers. In classes where every paper is graded, those students who consistently get high grades receive little specific feedback or encouragement to revise—doesn't an A paper imply perfection?

Christensen describes the impact of her grading approach on two very different writers: Mira, the class valedictorian who went on to teach writing at the university level, and Nicole, a struggling writer who didn't produce much until her second year with Christensen.

> In a mid-year class evaluation of my senior course . . . Nicole raised her hand. "I like that you don't grade our papers. I went through Sabin Elementary and Beaumont Middle Schools with Mira. Every time the teacher would hand back our papers, Mira's would have an A and mine would have a C. It made me feel like I wasn't as smart as Mira. Now when I look over at Mira's paper, I see that we both have comments from you written all over them. It's a conversation, not a competition."
>
> Mira, the valedictorian, also liked comments instead of grades. "What tells me more about my writing? A grade or the comments and questions you write in the margins?" In fact, Mira looked for colleges that wrote narrative evaluations of their students rather than grading them. (Now, she teaches writing at the college level and writes magnificent poetry.) (Christensen 2004–2005)

We have the same responsibility to respond thoughtfully and constructively to students who struggle and students who write well—helping them all to reach beyond what they can already do. In Christensen's policy, the value she places on context, improvement, and the ways in which process interacts with product is out in the open. Her policy is no dirty little secret, but a model for us all to consider.

Grading policies should not only help students to engage in the hard work of writing but should also encourage us to become better teachers. Policies that focus on process require teachers to foster insight into the writing process and provide opportunities for students to engage in it—they require us to *teach writing* rather than to simply assign, correct, and return essays. If we view our work as a series of prompts and corrections, we avoid thinking about the essence of language, thought, process, and the nature of learning. We avoid the difficult but rewarding work of setting up experiences that will lead to insightful, concise thinking and writing. According to Vygotsky (1962), thought and language are inextricable; writing and thinking support and build on each other. When our grading policies honor the development of thinking that leads to good writing, our grading promotes rather than undermines what we value.

Christensen's policy is point based, making it useful for teachers like my colleagues at the junior high who must hand out weekly grade strips. But not all grading policies that honor process must be based on points. My grading policy in my Personal Narratives class began with a description of my expectations in my course syllabus. I made a list of the activities I expected them to be engaged in: freewriting, discussing, revising, framing, reframing, exploring different avenues of the same idea, rehearsing, giving feedback, and so on. The course description itself began to show students what trust I placed in the creative process—they weren't being graded on the performance alone. This description of what I valued and wanted to teach began a conversation with students about the nature of creativity and the activities and experiences that lead to good writing.

Several times during the semester, I asked students to reflect on their participation and growth in the course. I would ask them to describe the writing and revisions they'd done, the conversations or thoughts that had prompted their writing or revisions, and the ways they'd gotten stuck and seen their way out of difficult spots. I'd ask them to summarize the feedback they'd gotten from various sources and to comment on that feedback; what had been helpful and why? I'd ask them to evaluate their participation, to identify their strengths and weaknesses and to describe a plan for what they'd work on in the coming weeks.

Periodically asking students to explain how they'd been engaged and what they had produced gave me the chance to talk to anyone at risk of failing the course—an opportunity that meets the objective behind distributing weekly grade strips. Students' evaluations were rarely different from mine, and several students did fail because they rarely came to class or didn't engage in thinking or writing much at all. But these periodic reflections gave students a chance to refocus on an aspect that they'd been ignoring, or with which they struggled. For instance, in the middle of the semester, Travers wrote that while he'd been thinking, talking, responding, and drawing quite a bit, he hadn't written anything substantive. He wondered what it was he had to say and vowed to work harder on getting his thoughts committed to paper. By the end of class, he wrote and performed an amazing scene based on his relationship with his father and their difficulty in saying what they felt. The conversational nature of the evaluation encouraged him to do something that was difficult on many levels for him, and refusing to rank every paper gave him and everyone in the classroom the freedom to think, talk, and write themselves into and out of risky corners—explorations that produced some of the most effective student writing I've ever read.

It was also important that I asked students to think about how their process was unique. Denni thought deeply and had many conversations with her friend Sarah before she wrote; these conversations did for her what Maria's tendency to combine different writings into more final versions of a draft did. We accomplish a deepening of our ideas in various ways, but without engaging in any activity to go beneath the surface of an idea, our writings tend toward one-dimensional cliché—an affliction devoutly to be avoided. Asking students how they approach this process shows not only that we expect them to engage, but that we trust them to do so in a way that fits their personalities, skills, and previous experiences. It also opens the door for us to suggest different approaches.

As long as grades or other forms of ranking are the ultimate goal of writing assessment, we will not truly be able to claim assessment for teaching and learning, as Brian Huot suggests that we must (2002a). But unless we begin experimenting in our classes with assessment in ways that honor our values about the complexities of the writing and responding process, we will never be in a position to call for the kind of paradigm shift that Yancey assures us is possible (1999). This experimentation and subversion or sidestepping of grades is no easy feat, but as long as reliability guides our values about writing assessment, why not have students stop writing altogether, forget all this blather about process and what working writers do, and bring back the highly reliable, relatively inexpensive multiple-choice grammar test? Unless we clarify, define, and begin acting on our values about writing assessment for ourselves, this is exactly what will happen.

How Do We Find Time to
Make It Meaningful?

And Other Questions About
Assessment Without Rubrics

My struggle with rubrics, Krystal's paper, the history of writing assessment, and the theories underlying how we teach and assess had thus far led me to approach teaching, responding, and grading in my classes differently. I was pleased with the results. I liked how the absence of predetermined categories allowed me to look for and encourage the incomplete but unique approaches that students were free to attempt without the fear of going against the rubric. I liked how the insight that our reactions are always based on assessment forced us to put our reactions more clearly into words. I liked how our acceptance of disagreement in assessment helped authors to clarify their purposes, sort through the biases that readers always bring to writing, and turn all of this disagreement and analysis into powerful revisions. I liked how the freedom from grading individual papers allowed students to take risks and write their way around subjects that were difficult but meaningful to them.

But how could my experience and approach translate into other classrooms? I had no desire to market The Maja Method® and go on tour or to force my sister and her colleagues to replace their mandatory classroom library arrangements with brightly colored wall-size laminated Disagreement in Response™ charts. In fact, I was convinced that my own way of assessing writing worked because it was responsive—evolving in the context of my search for answers and my students' needs—and I suspected that our model for how other teachers discover and create practices that work for them needed to be similarly responsive.

Still, when I would talk with my colleague Amy, she had many valid and interesting questions about how she might put some of these ideas about assessment to work in her own classroom. In fact, my conversations with her helped me to arrive at some of the practices that worked well for me. So in the spirit of starting a conversation that will lead us all toward more promising practices, I offer the essence of Amy's questions and a discussion of how I and other teachers might try to answer through our classroom practice. This conversation must continue well beyond the pages of this book. It is only when the conversation ends that we know we have settled for something less than what is possible.

You seem to be saying that giving up rubrics isn't truly effective unless we address how meaningful students' writing is to them. How do we make time to make it meaningful?

First of all, I don't view assessment as something we do *after* the writing process is complete. All writers assess writing as we go, hesitating slightly as we make judgments about what word works best or what ideas should come next. Every writing choice we make springs from some assessment that we've already made. Similarly, when we structure our writing classes, assessment should be woven throughout the writing process and be used for some end other than ranking—to help us make the series of choices that is our writing process. Assessment involves paying attention to the effects of our words, comparing that effect with our purposes, and using that comparison to try it differently. This is what Brian Huot might call "instructive assessment" (Huot 2002a).

One revelation in particular relieved my anxiety that my life would be overtaken by response to student writing: not all feedback and response need be written. During my first year of teaching, I was convinced that I needed to write long narratives in response to students' drafts. I wanted students to know that I'd paid attention to what they were trying to say and that I would work as hard as they did to help them write better. But this kind of response simply wasn't sustainable. However, I found that more important than a long-written response was a careful reading and sincere interest in helping students work through what they were trying to do. I found that I could accomplish this just as easily in a thirty-second conversation as a page-long written response.

In fact, I didn't write any of my responses to Maria's "Uniquely Me." I asked her questions about her work, she asked me questions, we talked, we argued, and the assessment happened in that conversation. Not only does this conversation relieve the burden of always writing our responses, but it is the means through which students find direction for their revisions, clarify their purposes, and argue with our assessments. I am thrilled when students challenge my suggestions or readings; unless the argument is about numbers or a grade, argument means that they are clarifying their purposes in writing and revisions, investing in the process instead of bowing to the teacher's idea of what their writing should be. Sometimes I even solicit their arguments. If I'm giving a suggestion or comment and notice hesitation in the student's face, I'll often say, "You look hesitant. Please argue with what I'm saying—this is *your* paper, and you have to make a decision that works for what you'd like to do." My goal isn't for them to follow my suggestion, but to learn to assess their work on their own. Arguing about the process of assessment allows them to take ownership of it.

In order to find time for these assessment conversations, I have to give students time to write in class. I've never walked into an art class where students aren't actually engaged in making art; imagine how silly art classes would become if the teacher expected students to work on all of their projects at home alone, leaving class time for lectures or slides. Of course we should expect students to write at home regularly. But assessment depends on observation, and if we do not allow students to write during class, we cannot observe their process or find the time to give them the responses and ask the questions that matter. While many teachers believe that it is important to write with students, I would rather observe and talk with students while they write. I still share my writing with students, but my time during their classes is devoted to them. This gives me several hours a week to engage in the most meaningful kind of assessment whether or not I write a word on their papers.

In addition, while I read everything that students write in class, I do not need to respond to everything. Students in my class keep a writer's journal, and I only respond to writing that I think has potential, making a quick note in the margins about something I find effective, or greeting a student who enters class with a comment such as, "Your questions about cloning made me think for a long time—have you thought about where you can go to find some answers?" The time I spend reading and responding to these journals is minimal, but these brief readings can be a powerful tool later in the writing process. For example, Jackson was in one of my eleventh-grade writing classes at the traditional high school. His writer's journal was mostly nondescript. But in the middle of many accounts of his day he described some old clay pipes that his father kept on a shelf. The description wasn't long, and I didn't write anything in response, but I was struck by the idea of the pipes and wondered what they were like. When we began to write personal narratives, Jackson claimed that his life was boring and that he had nothing to write about. I asked him about the pipes, and he began telling me about his father's relationship with his grandfather and how those pipes were symbolic of that. Someday those pipes would be his. All of a sudden, he had a powerful family relationship to write about with the most interesting of frames—clay pipes. In this brief conversation, Jackson had stumbled onto the beginning of a wonderful narrative that linked him to the men in his family.

Similarly, Sandy wrote a rambling paper about her father's birthday party. It was hard to follow and *long*. I didn't write a response because I wasn't sure where to begin; I wasn't pulled in by much of anything that she wrote—just one paragraph about how happy she was when she brought her dad the birthday cake. In class, I brought the paper to Sandy and said, "When I read your paper, the part I wanted to know more about was the moment you brought your dad the cake. Can you describe what was going on in your mind at that moment?" Sandy's eyes widened, and she began to talk about how this moment was the first birthday party she'd ever shared with her father. In fact, she'd met him for the first time only a week before the party. The conversation took two minutes. Sandy took her paper back and handed me a completely different and engaging narrative a week later about meeting her father for the first time—the paper she hadn't even known she'd wanted to write. The question and conversation did more to help her clarify her own thoughts than a written evaluation of "Focus—2, Organization—1."

The same is true of research papers. Carla was researching the origins of the Goth movement. Her introduction was riveting; she set up the problem she was about to investigate beautifully. And she did a wonderful job of tracing symbolism in the movement and showing how and why Edgar Allen Poe was credited as a founding father. She ran into trouble when she tried to describe why people start getting involved; her paper wandered into abstractions that lost my attention. As she walked into class, I pulled her aside and asked her if she had any friends who identified with the Goth movement. When she nodded, I suggested that she interview them and use their stories to make the last section of her paper more interesting. She agreed, and began an important revision. This conversation, based on my assessment of her first draft, took all of thirty seconds.

Another revelation that relieved the burden for me was that mine was not the only response that mattered. I encourage students to get feedback from a variety of sources: parents, peers, anyone willing to listen. When we were working on descriptive writing, my ninth-grade students who live in the rural Midwest wrote to my sister's students in New York City describing their town and lives in it. Letter writing to real people (as opposed to the audience implied in many standardized testing prompts) includes a natural feedback loop. Not only were my students hungry for responses—Nina asked me every day if more letters had come—but if students wrote something unclear, their writing partners asked clarifying questions or made comments based on the wrong assumptions. Either way, my students knew if their words had communicated as they'd intended. Through this exchange of writing, my students were motivated to see their own town differently—they were stunned that an apartment in my sister's neighborhood could cost $2,000 a month. Likewise, my sister's students were amused that our downtown consists of three main streets and that our tallest building is four stories high. Through getting to know their audience's assumptions, my students framed their descriptions differently; they couldn't take anything about their lives for granted. This experience not only strengthened their descriptive writing skills, but also prepared them to understand the perspective shifts that Scout goes through in *To Kill a Mockingbird*, which we would read later in the year.

But how do you find other people to read and respond to your students' work?

I was lucky that my sister taught in New York City. Not everyone has a built-in cross-country teaching partner. But there are many ways to connect with interested teachers from all over the country. Professional listservs are an invaluable resource for cultivating teaching and response partners. Dawn Hogue and Pat Schulze met on NCTE's English email list. Pat taught in North Dakota and Dawn taught in Wisconsin, but they discovered that they both had an interest in multigenre writing and developed an oral history writing unit together through developing a website that their classes shared, *www.sheboyganfalls.k12.wi.us/cyberenglish9/Oral_history/oh_main.htm*. Their students interviewed an older relative or neighbor about an experience in some historical event, researched that event, and posted their writings on the Web. Students read these essays to the person they'd interviewed, and gained invaluable responses about whether they'd gotten it right or missed something. In addition, since they all had access to the Web, Pat and Dawn's students gave each other feedback, asked and answered each other's questions, and shared successes and failures.

I did a similar project with my students and residents at a local nursing home. We didn't partner with another class, but the nursing home residents themselves provided the audience and feedback. Students worked especially hard on their writing because they'd established relationships with the men and women they'd interviewed. They frequently read drafts in progress to their interview partners, asking if they'd missed anything, making sure they'd gotten details right. At the end of the writing process, the students received more encouragement and reinforcement that audience matters. Brian got a letter from one of the resident's granddaughters in Oklahoma; she'd heard about the project and wanted to add the student's writing to a geneology project she was working on. Another student got a letter from his interview partner's son who was the principal of a school in Texas. He had heard about what we were doing and wanted to know if the student would describe the project so that students at his school could do a similar project. Another woman we'd never met wrote to us to say that our visits were making her mother very happy and gave her reason to get up in the morning. Dan's interview partner stopped by the school occasionally to check up on him and came to his graduation.

Ted Nellen, who has been teaching Cyber-English classes for over twenty years in New York City public schools, uses technology to widen the audience and generate more feedback for his scholars. Ted teaches all of his English classes online. Scholars create their own Web pages, post all of their writing online, and use online writing mentors—any interested person willing to read and respond to their writing. To help the writing mentors respond meaningfully, Ted's resource page for mentors, http://www.tnellen.com/method.html directs telementors to respond in three simple ways.

I heard...

As a reviewer, first try to summarize what you think the piece was about. This is the easy part. Tell the writer what you saw as the story or the main idea. As a writer, listen to this section, and try to hear whether or not you communicated what you were trying to communicate.

I noticed . . .

As a reviewer, tell the author about some of the things that attracted your attention. What worked well? What details seemed especially vivid or striking? What will you remember about this paper? As a writer, think about why the reviewer noticed these things, and how you can make all your writing as effective.

I wondered . . .

As a reviewer, did you have any questions when you finished reading? Did you not understand what something meant, or why it was included? Did something bother or disturb you? Did you suspect something might have worked better another way? This section is your chance to ask the writer all these questions. As a writer, try to answer the reviewer's questions. Look at your writing again, and see if there is any way to make those points clearer to a reader.

These questions focus response on the rhetorical nature of writing, asking readers to explain how the writing affects them rather than to rate the paper's organization, ideas, or mechanics.

Colleges of education are another valuable resource for widening our students' audience. Think of your own writing methods courses: wouldn't it have been nice to actually have student writing in all its messy glory to work with and refer to? If pre-student teachers developed a semester-long writing and response relationship with each of your students, imagine the benefit to both. The pre-student teacher would be able to bring questions and dilemmas with your students to his or her methods class and instructor, and your students would have one more interested party to learn from.

My students have a hard enough time getting past "I liked it" in peer revision sessions. How do you teach students and even other interested readers how to make their responses to writing into a helpful response?

I'm excited about the possibilities to tie the study of literature to the way that we teach students to respond to each other's writing. When I teach a book, I try to engage students in many levels of response to the text. I ask students to connect their experience and observations about the world around them to what they read, to describe an author's style, to point out passages that they like or that confuse them. It seems to me that this same way of reading can apply to how we read each other's writing. In fact, Brian Huot claims that "using assessment to teach writing...means teaching the process of assessment, and this means teaching them how to read and to describe what they have read" (2002b, 177).

If we start with the assumption that we should read our students' writing in the same way we read literature, we can borrow many of the methods we use to teach reading and response. For instance, to tease apart the difference between a quick reaction and the articulation of that reaction, I begin by asking my class to write a list of ten things they've read in the past year. Then, in a class brainstorm, I ask them to describe the ways that they feel while they are reading something: bored, curious, engaged, angry, frustrated, and so on. If the brainstorm takes a while to get started, I will tell a story about my own reaction to reading something in a literature class, usually focusing on a time that reading frustrated me since they don't expect me to have this reaction—after all, I'm the English teacher!

Once we have a good list, I ask students to pick several of these words that they can relate to—perhaps *bored* and *frustrated*—and then ask them to remember something specific they read that prompted these reactions. Then, I ask them to think about why they felt that way—what about the text and their own circumstances contributed to that reaction? If students phrase the reasons for their reactions in a particularly interesting way, I write it down in order to discuss it further. Once we have an interesting list of reactions and reasons for those reactions, the stage is set for how students need to respond to each other's work. For instance, one student said that he always zoned out when the author went into "lecture mode." This began an interesting discussion of ways to avoid lecture mode in my research writing class. I now regularly look for examples of how contemporary writers avoid lecture mode and bring these to the class for discussion. In the November 2005 issue of *The Atlantic Monthly*, P.J. O'Rourke tries to describe how the Airbus A380, a mammoth new passenger plane, is built. The beginning of this description almost loses me, but O'Rourke pulls me quickly back into the article through use of humor and empathy.

> The wing panels are up to 108 feet long and nine feet wide, and in places they are only an eigth of an inch thick. They need to hold a "double curved aerodynamic shape." The way to achieve this is with a twenty-four-hour application of varying temperatures and loads to create "stress relaxation" and "permanent deformation." The process

is called "creep age forming," and opportunities for wisecracks about Michael Jackson aside, I have no idea what I'm talking about.

But Charles Champion did. And he made everything, if not exactly clear, clearly exciting. (177)

When I brought this portion of the article to my class, not only did students immediately notice Rourke's use of first person, but they also began thinking about when empathizing with the reader might help them lead their reader through difficult material. In a subsequent peer-revision session, I heard John tell Josh that his paper about string theory went into lecture mode too often, and Josh responded by saying that perhaps the empathy strategy might work well in his case, since he truly did empathize with the reader; he laughed as he admitted that string theory was almost impossible for anyone to understand.

These insights about writing weren't engendered by single-minded focus on ideas, form, flavor, mechanics, and wording. Instead, they came about because we were focused on the rhetorical purpose of writing and we talked through what happens in our minds when we read. As teachers, we may fear setting aside "scientifically endorsed" insights about writing; what if we don't have any of our own insights? But if we're invested readers and writers and if we encourage our students to be invested readers and writers, we are bound to stumble onto the kind of revelations that move us forward rather than holding us back.

My students are used to trusting the teacher to respond to and judge their writing. With all of this possibly divergent response, how do you teach students how to deal with it?

Now is the time for a graphic organizer! Except now we aren't using the matrix to reduce the qualities of good writing; this time, we're using it to keep track of who says what, why they say it, and what the writer decides to do as a result of all of this feedback. For example, feedback to early versions of my introduction and first paragraph might look like Figure 8–1.

Of course, the graphic organizer itself isn't important; the idea of finding insight in disagreement is. After discussing the importance of articulating their disagreements about assessing each other's work with students in my research writing course, I watched Emma, Jesse, and Katie talk about Emma's paper. Inspired by her experiences babysitting a toddler named Eddy who could not yet speak, Emma had researched and written about causes and treatments of developmental speech

	Dealing with Disagreement in Response		
Reader	**Summary of Comments or Areas of Concern**	**Reason for Comment or Concern**	**Information About the Reader**
Patrick	Didn't like the story at the beginning of the introduction.	Thought it meandered, "Shouldn't *rubric* be your first word?"	A psychologist
Amy	Liked the introduction.	Was pulled in by the story—could relate and picture the whole thing.	A writing teacher
Bob	Liked the introduction but didn't feel it belonged in the beginning before mention of rubrics.	Slowed down the reading—anxious to get to the "meat."	An expert in writing assessment
Lind	Liked the introduction where it was.	Felt "primed and ready to go."	A writing teacher

Figure 8–1 *Dealing with Disagreement in Response*

delays. After reading the paper with the group, Katie mentioned how much she loved the section in the paper that described symptoms of speech difficulties. As Katie raved about the section, I could see Jesse withdraw, partially covering some comments she'd written on her copy of Emma's paper. I stepped in and asked Jesse if she disagreed with Katie's enthusiasm. She looked sheepishly at Emma and admitted that she'd been totally lost in that section. As they tried to figure out why they reacted so differently to the same words, Katie revealed that as she read the symptoms of speech delays, she could just picture Eddy pointing and grunting. Jesse came to life, asking if Katie knew the same child that Emma knew. When Katie revealed that they both babysat for Eddy, Jesse said, "That's why you get it and I don't! You know the kid, so your mind fills in the details. I don't know the kid, and so I don't fill in the gaps. She hasn't actually written down what she means." Jesse turned to Emma. "Why don't you just describe Eddy as you talk about the symptoms, and that way, I'll see what you two see when you read it."

Katie's affirmation without Jesse's confusion would never have led to an important revision for Emma, but Jesse's confusion without Katie's revelation of their shared experience of Eddy's behavior would never have pointed the way toward a solution. Through disagreement and articulation of what happened in their minds as they read, Katie and Jesse helped Emma not only to identify a weakness in her writing, but also helped her to fix it. Their differing assessments, grounded in their admittedly subjective readings, helped Emma's writing to improve. Assessment, at last, reclaimed for teaching and learning!

Sometimes, the information about the reader that might help a student deal with disagreement might be something like, "Pat is bored by everything. I've never seen her interested in a book or anything anyone is reading. I'm not too concerned that she thought my paper was boring." This process puts the student ultimately in charge of assessment—they are in the position of assessing the assessments. In fact, the teacher's assessment might be one among many, but it is up to the student to determine how much weight to give that assessment. Since they are ultimately the ones responsible for their own words, this transfer of the teacher's power to them is critical.

I'm still nervous to give up rubrics altogether, since I still need to familiarize my students with the rubrics against which they'll be judged by the state, and since I've always used rubrics.

Our ideals will always be in conflict with reality, but it is this tension that moves us forward or keeps us from slipping backward. I haven't found a way to make writing in every class for every student meaningful always. And there have been times when I've used rubrics because I wasn't sure how else to structure what I was trying to do. But my vision of what writing and assessment *can* be keeps me honest; the things I do in desperation may be forgivable, but they don't do justice to what I know about the nature of thinking, learning, and writing. If we trust the writing process to guide students surely but unevenly toward product, we should trust our own teaching process—giving ourselves permission to fail, but viewing and reflecting on those failures in light of our values and ideals. How will we help students to wield words in ways that unleash the magnificent, transformative power of language? Failure to meet the ideal is par for the course, but being guided by any other question won't do.

References

Anson, C., ed. 1989. *Writing and Response: Theory, Practice, and Research.* Urbana, IL: NCTE.

Applebee, A. 1974. *Tradition and Reform in the Teaching of English.* Urbana, IL: NCTE.

Broad, B. 2003. *What We Really Value: Beyond Rubrics in Teaching and Assessing Writing.* Logan: Utah State University Press.

Caruano, R. 1999. "An Historical Overview of Standardized Educational Testing in the United States." Online: *www.gwu.edu /~gjackson/caruano.PDF.*

Christensen, L. 2004–2005. "Moving Beyond Judgment" *Rethinking Schools* 19 (2): 33–37.

Christenbuy, L., A. Gere, and K. Sassi. 2005. *Writing on Demand: Best Practices and Strategies for Success.* Portsmouth, NH: Heinemann.

Daiker, D. 1989. "Learning to Praise." In *Writing and Response,* edited by Chris Anson, 103–13. Urbana, IL: NCTE.

Diederich, P., J. French, and S. Carlton. 1961. "Factors in Judgments of Writing Ability." *Educational Testing Service Research Bulletin* 61: 15.

Durm, M. 1993. "A History of Grading." *The Educational Forum* 57(X):XX–XX. Online: *www.indiana.edu/~educy520/sec6342 /week_07/durm93.pdf*

Educational Testing Service. DATE. "Frequently Asked Questions About Criterion." Online: *www.ets.org/criterion/elementary/faq.html.*

Ekstrom, R. 1964. "Colleges' Use and Evaluation of the CEEB Writing Sample." *Educational Testing Service Research Bulletin* 64: 4.

French, J. 1962. "Schools of Thought in Judging Excellence of English Themes." Paper presented at invitational conference on testing problems, 1961. Princeton, NJ: Educational Testing Services.

Frisch-Kowalski, S. 2003. "The SAT: A Timeline of Changes." New York: College Entrance Examinations Board. Online: *www.collegeboard.com/prod_downloads/sat/techhandbook/chapter4.pdf.*

Gorrell, K. 1998. NCTE listserv. Nov 1, 1998.

Hook, J. N. 1979. *A Long Way Together: A Personal View of NCTE's First Sixty-Seven Years.* Urbana, IL: NCTE.

Horning, K. 2001. "The Editor Who Discovered the Stars." *School Library Journal* Online: *www.schoollibraryjournal.com/article/CA90684.html.*

Hubin, D. R. 1988. *The Scholastic Aptitude Test: Its Development and Introduction, 1900–1948.* Doctoral dissertation. University of Oregon.

Huot, B. 2002a. *(Re)Articulating Writing Assessment for Teaching and Learning.* Logan: Utah State University Press.

Huot, B. 2002b. "Toward a New Discourse of Assessment for the College Writing Classroom." *College English* 65 (2): 163–80.

Janis, I. 1982. *Groupthink.* 2d ed. Boston: Houghton Mifflin.

Lawson, B., S. S. Ryan, and W. Winterowd. 1989. *Encountering Student Texts: Interpretive Issues in Reading Student Writing.* Urbana, IL: NCTE.

Lazerson, M. 2001. *A Faithful Mirror.* New York: The College Board. Online: *www.collegeboard.com/faithfulmirror/pdfs/faithful_mirror_379_398.pdf.*

Lunsford, A. 1986. "The Past—and Future—of Writing Assessment." In *Writing Assessment: Issues and Strategies,* edited by K. Greenberg, H. Wiener, and E. Donovan, pp 1–12. New York and London: Longman.

Lynne, P. 2004. *Coming to Terms: A Theory of Writing Assessment.* Logan: Utah State University Press.

Marsh, Amy. 2004. Personal communication. 29 Dec. 2004.

Michigan Educational Assessment Program. 2005. "High School English Language Arts Test Booklet, Form 1." State Administrative Board, State of Michigan.

Moss, P. 1994. "Can There Be Validity Without Reliability?" *Educational Researcher* 23 (2): 5–12.

Northwest Regional Educational Laboratory. 2005. "6+1 Trait® Scoring Continuum." Online: *www.nwrel.org/assessment/pdfRubrics/6plus1traits.PDF.*

O'Rourke, P. J. 2005. "The Mother Load." *The Atlantic Monthly.* 296 (4): 170–178.

Patterson, Nancy. 2005. Personal communication. 5 March 2005.

Peake, Leigh. 2005. Phone and email communication.

Reid, Louann. Email communication. 2005. 18 June 2005.

Salary.com. 2005. "Salary Wizard." Online: *www.salary.com*

Spandel, V. 2005. *The 9 Rights of Every Writer*. Portsmouth, NH: Heinemann.

Tchudi, S., ed. 1997. *Alternatives to Grading Student Writing*. Urbana, IL: NCTE.

Vygotsky, L. 1962. *Thought and Language*. Translated by Eugenia Hanfman and Gertrude Vakar. Cambridge, MA: MIT Press.

Washington Post Educational Forum. 2002. "Dad Tweaked Paragraph Three."

Williams, Lind. 2005a. Email communication. 17 Feb. 2005.

Williams, Lind. 2005b. Heinemann Reader Report. 7 Feb. 2005.

Yancey, K. B. 1999. "Looking Back as We Look Forward: Historicizing Writing Assessment." *College Composition and Communication* 50: 483–501.

Zemelman, S., H. Daniels, and A. Hyde. 1998. *Best Practice: New Standards for Teaching and Learning in America's Schools*. Portsmouth, NH: Heinemann.

Zimmerman, Kristi. Personal communication. 23 Feb. 2005.

Index